MW00905350

The
Successful
Woman

First edition

Printed in 2002

Copyright © 2002 by Kathy Glover Scott M.S.W.

All rights reserved. No part of this book may be used or reproduced in any manner whatsoever without written permission of the Author. Exception: a reviewer or researcher who may quote brief passage in a review or research document with full credit given to the Author.

For additional information to contact the author, visit:

http//: www.kathygloverscott.com

or

http//: the successfulwoman.com

Cataloguing Information

Glover Scott M.S.W., Kathy 1958-

Full title: The Successful Woman

Descriptive Information: A program that opens the door to your limitless potential.

ISBN 0-9684450-3-9

    1.   Self-help for women

    2.   Women who work and in business – self-employed

This book is a tool to assist you with the success (as you define it) in your life. Kathy Glover Scott is not responsible for any outcomes as a result of using the information in this book.

Dedicated with love and gratitude
to my teacher and friend
Ann Thomas

The Successful Woman
Table of Contents

With Gratitude vii
Introduction ix

Chapter 1: Creating An Inner Foundation 1
    Birthing A New Life 3
    Shifting Our Perspective 4
    Healthy Selfishness 5
    Owning Our Qualities. 8
    Exercise: Owning Your Qualities. 9

Chapter 2: Redefining Success for Women. 15
    The Meaning of Success. 16
    The Outdated 20th Century Model of Success. 20
    The New Model of Success for Women 22
    Success Tips for the 21st Century Woman. 27
    Exercise: Boosting Your Focus on Success 32

Chapter 3: 'Energy Choicing' in Daily Life 35
    The F.A.S.T. Model for Understanding Energy 37
    What is Energy Choicing?. 39
    The New Approach – Energy Choicing. 41
    Exercise: Five Questions for Smarter Choices. 47

Chapter 4: Stress and Self-Care in Women's Lives. 51
    Stress and Success. 52
    Understanding the Stress Down-Line 55
    Keys to Decreasing the Stress That's Self-Created 56
    Exercise: Eliminating Tunnel Vision 58
    Stress, Success and Self-Care. 58
    Blocks to Building a Self-Care Attitude 65
    Instant Self-Care Skills. 69
    Exercise: Energizing Your Self-Care Attitude 71

Chapter 5: Eliminating Self-Defeating Thinking that Blocks Success **73**

The Outcome of Self-Defeating Thinking 74

Becoming an Observer of Your Own Thought Process 78

The Eight Most Common Patterns for Women.......... 81

Exercise #1: Accelerating Your Observational Abilities.... 85

Exercise #2: Reducing Self-Defeating Thinking 87

Chapter 6: Self-Coaching and the Power of Limitless Thinking **89**

Keys to Becoming Your Own Self-Coach............... 90

Exercise: Strategies for Developing Self-Supportive Statements 92

Exercise: Transforming Your Thought Patterns.......... 94

The Power of Limitless Thinking 96

Expand Your Thoughts to Expand Your Potential........ 99

Exercise: Recharging Through Your Daydreams 101

10 Keys to Limitless Thinking for Women............. 103

Chapter 7: Owning Our Emotional Strengths **107**

Beliefs About Feeling............................. 111

Proactively Experiencing Your Emotions.............. 115

Exercise: Overcoming Fear......................... 124

Guilt and How to Conquer It 126

Exercise: Undergoing Guilt's Power 131

Chapter 8: Intuition and Personal Power.......... **133**

Recognizing and Experiencing Intuition.............. 135

The Benefits of Strengthened Intuition 138

10 Truths about Intuition 141

Self-Talk for Expanding Intuition 142

Keys to Jump-Starting Your Intuition................ 151

Creativity and Success in Your Life 152

Exercise: Igniting Your Creativity 155

Chapter 9: Abundance, Prosperity and Success...... **157**

Living in the 'Joy Frequency'....................... 158

Reveling in the Abundance in Your Life Now.......... 159

The Meaning of Money & The Prosperity Process....... 164

Exercise: Attaining Your Goals Through Imagery....... 167

In Conclusion............................... **174**

With Gratitude

The Successful Woman is the outcome of several years of teaching, learning, integrating and writing. It is also the outcome of a lifetime spent with amazing women and men. With gratitude, I would like to acknowledge a few of them who are a part of this book.

To the women who have attended my seminars, presentations, groups and shared their souls and struggles with me – thank-you. You number in the thousands, yet each of you have touched my soul and have contributed to this book.

For my life partner, Craig Scott: both my computer and I thank you with all our being. My children have been the greatest life teachers for me. Thomas and Tegan, you have brought the greatest blessing to my life.

My life is rich and abundant. I would like to thank the following people for 'being there' and assisting in their own ways with the writing of The Successful Woman. To the women of my birth family: particularly my Mom (Bev McCutcheon) and my sisters Ruth, Mary and Carolyn; my aunt and godmother Gayle Broad and my great Aunt Margaret. There are many members in my chosen family, but particularly Adele Alfano, Samantha Abel, Dawn Massiah, Lisa Zaretsky, Daye Sutherland, Ann Thomas, Cheryl Fleming and Olive Schisler.

My gratitude also goes to: Angela Tortolo and Peter DeShane of the Healthquest Center in London, Ontario, members of the Canadian Association of Professional Speakers (and especially the Southwestern Ontario Chapter), Dan Poynter of Parapublishing, Maureen Geddes of Cangram International, the staff of Double Q Printing in London, Dian Vail of the Women's Conference, Sandy Ross of WordsWorth and Paulette O'Neil of Partners in Health.

For me, being a Successful Woman comes from living a spiritually based life. Words cannot express my thankfulness to God for bringing all these amazing people into my life and for the spiritual guidance that I have received. Blessed be!

*- **Kathy Glover Scott***

Introduction

As women, we are finally beginning to say, "I am deserving". These words may pass through your mind as a fleeting thought, or you may say them to a friend. You may even shout them from a mountaintop! Know that once you own the possibility of 'being deserving', your life begins to unfold in a new and amazing way.

Do you ever feel the ache deep inside you to be more than you see yourself as being right now? Do you ever want to scream at those around you " I am more than what you see – please see the real me"? Do you ever experience the inner struggle of being all you know that you can be, yet feel swallowed up by the demands of daily life? And do you remain silent, moving through each day doing what seems to be the right thing to do, and ignoring that inner, compelling voice urging you to change direction, change course, and live a life that has real meaning for you?

If any of this reverberates deep inside of you, then you are on the path of being a truly *Successful Woman*. This inner conflict is the catalyst for becoming all you can be. This inner angst leads to the unfolding of self, and being 'successfully you' does not occur without working and living in a new way.

This book is about success for women – success as defined by you and at whatever stage you are at in your life. To be successful, what you pursue and how you pursue it needs to be in alignment with who you are. This connection creates an amazing link to your inner gifts; intuition, creativity, focus and personal power and lays the foundation for good health, prosperity, mental wellness and inner peace. The Successful Woman is a tool to accelerate your personal growth in a way that keeps the real you alive and in the forefront in your life, living fully from this relationship with yourself and allowing everything else in life to flow from it.

As the author, I am a woman with a young family, a home, a business and all of the joys and challenges of daily life. This book is written by a woman who lives the same day-to-day realities of life that you do. I've been teaching what you will find in this book for several years to thousands of women and have received tremendous feedback about the successes women have attained through integrating these approaches in their lives.

This is not a book about coping or managing your life. This is a book about transformation. It is about moving out of merely coping and surviving in your life on a day-to-day basis. It is about moving to living a life where your 'optimal self' – with her limitlessness, inner peace, creativity and wisdom is how you thrive each day. You deserve to live feeling less fragmented with all the amazing aspects of who you are fully visible and expressed. And this flows through shifting your perspective about yourself.

Imagine this picture. Take your hand and reach down inside yourself and when you pull your hand out, you are holding the real you. She needs and desires to be fully visible in the world each and every day. Pull her up to the light and let her breathe and love and express and create and be prosperous and feel truly connected to others. Let her feel focused and joyful and purposeful. Let her live on the outside of you each and every day. Check in with your body – are you feeling some anxiety? If you are, it's normal – you are choosing to explore the potential of living the life that you deserve. Now look below the anxiety – go beneath this layer of fear that is not really real. Connect with the deep sense of relief that you have in reading these words – in reading that there is a way out of yourself to live in the flow of what is good and right for you. This book is a roadmap for you.

It is time that we move past coping. As women we have been doing this for about 10,000 years. Coping is how we have learned to view our lives and, in turn, have silenced our dreams and desires. The energy of coping is aligned with survival. The inner belief is that if I can cope, then I can survive. This book will lead you to leave this belief behind and open your vision to your own limitless potential with a sense of inner peace without guilt.

Isn't it interesting how the right things in life come along at the right time? As women, we hold the energy that will transform our world and, yes, save this planet. And this energy will only be released through developing a strong relationship with ourselves and owning how powerful and amazing we are. It will only come through defining success in our terms. We are powerful and limitless - and you will learn that this power has nothing to do with controlling others. The only way for this amazing force to be released is through looking at success in life from a very personal perspective that flows from your soul self.

*- **Kathy Glover Scott, M.S.W.***

It never occurs to me that there are things I can't do.

- Whoopi Goldberg, actor

Chapter 1

Creating an Inner Foundation

Being successful in your own life is a very powerful place for a woman to be.

We are living in very unique times. On one hand, women have limitless potential. On the other hand, women have never been so challenged emotionally, mentally, physically and spiritually. This enables a paradox to be created - one that lives inside of each and every woman today. Do you ever experience this inner conflict? On one hand, you feel the overwhelming desire to grow, to fully and openly express yourself and to reach for the stars. On the other hand, you feel so stressed and worn out that your desires and goals turn into frustrations. When you do attain them, the joy is limited and you do not feel very important in your own life.

Living a life from your core of strength and power comes through moving from an externally to an internally experienced life. Now, we live our lives mainly based on the needs, desires and demands of the others in our lives. We live feeling pulled through each day and at the end of the parade, rather than leading through each day at the beginning. We are not even aware of the depth that our needs, desires and wants are colored and controlled by the needs, desires and wants of our children, spouses, partners, bosses, co-workers, parents, siblings – the list can be endless. It takes a courageous woman to say 'it is time to move from an externally ruled life to one that I lead from my own inner foundation.'

It takes courage, yet it has never been easier. The reason is that over the past couple of years women have begun as a group to say 'I am deserving'. This is an incredibly powerful statement. Try it out for yourself by going to a mirror and looking directly at yourself. Say "I am Deserving" in a strong tone of voice while looking at yourself straight in the eye. Do it several times. If you find it a challenge to hold your gaze and keep your tone of voice constant, you are not alone. This is new for us, yet your real self wants to yell it from a mountaintop for the entire world to hear.

You see, over the past 30 years, life for all of us has shifted dramatically, with women moving in to the work world as a force of change. The shift has not only affected your life, but the lives of everyone in it. And for women whose primary work is in the home, the demands and challenges have rapidly accelerated in your life as well. Over the past 30 years, we have been trying to figure out 'how to do it right'. Our energies have been focused on trying to work and be productive in many different areas of our lives at the same time. And now we are admitting that it does not work for us the way we have been doing it!

Admitting that it doesn't work is not an easy thing, for many of us have learned to buy-in to having a 'perfection attitude'. This means that 'I have to be able to do it all, do it well and convince others that I am doing it all, doing it well and really making it all look easy.' This illusion has created suffering in women's lives. You may think 'suffering' is a very strong word, yet it is the correct one to use. Suffering in your body, your mind, your emotions and most importantly, suffering in your spirit that leads to a disconnection from who you are and what you really need.

Birthing A New Life

Think of it this way. We have come through the birthing of our new lives as women with greater choices and a vision of our limitless potential. This was not a vision that many of our mothers or the amazing women before her could ever consider. They did not have the concepts or permission to even think about living life the way we do, or with the potential for choice and personal growth that we have. This birthing process has been difficult for us as it is all new. The women before us could not have taught us how to live life as we do, with the expanded horizons and daily challenges. People in the future will look back on our time as an era of incredible change with regard to technology, communications, science and the creation of energy. Yet, the people of the future will hold in awe the social and spiritual shifts that have occurred and the new order that we have created.

We are pioneers of a new era for living. As women, we are the center of our families and communities. Some people may disagree with this, yet it is true. We are the foundations for our families and our family units are the foundations for our communities, nations and the global village that technology has allowed us to create.

You are the Center, You are the Core and You are the Future.

As women, we know this deep inside ourselves, which at times leaves us feeling more tired and feeling that we have the weight of the world on our shoulders. It is necessary now for us to shift how we have been living our lives. Being fragmented and exhausted ourselves enables the fragmentation and exhaustion of our planet to continue.

Try not to jump to feeling guilt! It is really easy for us to shift into believing that we are not doing enough whenever an issue is identified. We jump to a very personal place of self-blame and feeling like we are not good enough. And, as long as we continue to do this, as women, we will never live from the core of strength and personal power that each and every one of us has.

"I am deserving!" Such powerful words, as they will be the ones that will lead you and I through the shift of being all that we can be. They are the words that will lead us to having healthier lives for ourselves, to own our roles as leaders in our families and communities and to enable the real harmonious nature of our planet to emerge. Learning how to say these words – to live these words – with clarity and conviction is the journey that we are on with this book and in our lives.

Shifting Our Perspective

For the past 10,000 years, women have lived their lives in a fairly consistent way. Our role as primary caregivers in our homes and for our families has remained the same. So today, we are living a view of our lives and ourselves that is very firmly entrenched in our beliefs and value systems. It is how we have learned to live within each cell of our bodies. To move to living with a new foundation for how you see yourself and how you live life requires a major shift in attitude.

What you think and believe about yourself creates the life that you live. Simple as that, yet so complex to grasp! How you perceive yourself deep in your core leads to how you do everything during each and everyday. Your understanding of this will unfold as you work through this book. This shift in perspective about yourself is a process of undoing old learning and integrating new learning in to your life. Your first reaction to this may be "I don't have enough time or energy for any new learning. Just tell me how to do it a new way." The reality is that people can tell you 'how-to' but real learning and change comes can only take root and grow through your self. The goal is to become more in charge of your own life, and if you rely on someone else to tell you how to do it, you are continuing to give your power and wisdom away.

This process of shifting comes from within yourself through the new perspective about yourself that you are choosing. And the first step is to move from having an external view of your life to having an internal one. In other words, it is about having a 'healthy selfishness'. When you do live in a 'healthy self-centered' way:

▸▸ You begin to live a life that has real meaning for you

▸▸ You become more focused and attain your goals more easily, and

▸▸ Your are less affected emotionally, mentally and physically by stress.

Healthy Selfishness

Today, with our real selves wanting to be 'let out' and the drive to live the life we deserve, there is a real push to build a stronger relationship with ourselves. We crave this from the marrow of our bones; yet fear it at the same time. This fear comes from a deep source inside ourselves, one that is built upon years of learning about who I am 'supposed to be' as a woman.

As women, we learned early in life that we need to put the concerns, needs, goals, desires and dreams of others before our own. Some women get this message more strongly than others, but it has been a part of how we have been socialized. The remedy to this is developing a 'healthy selfishness' through building a stronger relationship with yourself and letting you be the focal point of your life around which everything and everyone else revolves.

A fear we have as women is to live life with an "I" perspective rather than living as we do now: based on the needs and desires of others. At every party, isn't there always that one person who can corner you and talk about no-one but themselves and their life? They have no real interest in you or your life - they only want an audience for themselves. Our fear as women in moving to healthy selfishness is that we will become that person! Don't worry, this will not happen! Could you even imagine shifting so profoundly from a life where you give so much love and nurturing to others to one where it is non-existent?

In fact, by learning to be self-centred in a healthy way, you automatically find that you become more focused, productive, and stress will begin to have less control in your life. Healthy selfishness leads you to feeling more in charge of your life, even though the demands continue around you. You are able to make better choices in how you work, and use your energy that turns on the 'success magnet' that is already inside of you.

> **This relationship with self must be the strongest relationship in your life, and the most protected.**

This relationship is about owning all of who you are and the amazing gifts that you bring to each and every situation or experience each and every day. It is about developing a personal trust with the knowledge that you rely on yourself and your own judgment as the guiding force in your life. And through this trust, you really experience the depth and breadth of the core of strength inside of you, and lead from this even when life challenges hit you all at once.

This relationship with yourself opens the door to:

➤ Knowing that your life has real meaning for you.

➤ Valuing yourself and your uniqueness.

➤ Knowing that those in your life genuinely value you and your uniqueness.

➤ Becoming a Success Magnet for yourself in your own life.

Through the course of this book, these four factors will be explained and taught in depth. You'll begin to feel them grow inside yourself, becoming more and more a part of how you live each day. You will naturally begin to treat yourself in a lighter, more loving way, and then this flows like ripples on a pond to others in your life. As your energy changes, past behaviors and attitudes that may have blocked success in your life fall away. A light is ignited inside of you – a beacon – that attracts positive experiences, healthier relationships, abundance and success.

The 'Human Doing' and the 'Human Being'

Stress has an incredible impact on everyone's life, but particularly so for women. Stress does impact our ability to create a strong relationship with self. The daily stress that we experience creates a duality and separates us from our own true nature. If you have been feeling like two different people who are both pulled in many directions, you are not alone. The one part of you is the **Human Doing**. She is the one who goes non-stop during the day, almost always thinking of others and what needs to get done. She is very good at blaming herself when things do not flow smoothly. The other part of you is the **Human Being**. She desires two things:

1) To live a more balanced life, and

2) To have genuine connection with herself and the significant others in her life.

She wants to express her talents, gifts and creativity in a way that does not have regular expression in the Human Doing world. Do you ever find yourself feeling angry and depressed, especially around the people in your life with who you want to be at your best? Do you find that they often get the worst of you? This is common in our lives today, and a reality based on being two people living in one body trying to get everything done, while at the same time walking around feeling guilty and often inadequate.

Imagine the Human Being part of you standing off to the side watching the Human Doer all day long. Once in a while, she finds a way to express herself and the gifts that she really wants to give the world.

More often than not, she waits in the wings hoping to be noticed and embraced, and become a regular part of your life. When she is let in regularly, life is actually lived more smoothly. The feeling of being continually fragmented throughout the day is reduced. You no longer feel like you are running all day trying to catch up with yourself.

> Starting this reunion of the Human Being and Doing begins with owning your qualities.

Owning Our Qualities

Qualities are the essence of who we are. They are those characteristics and attributes which are distinct to you, and make up the one-of-a-kind person that you are. Each and every one of us brings our own special magic to everything we do and everyone we meet during the day. They are our strengths. Owning our qualities and letting them flow freely enables our sense of personal power and being in charge to grow and flourish in our daily lives.

Qualities are Who a person Is – not What she does.

The value system today expects people to be Human Doings rather than Human Beings. We have learned to define ourselves by what we do during the day, how much we accomplish at it, and how busy we are. This process supports us having low self-esteem and confidence. When a person's esteem is low, we actually try to hide our uniqueness and strengths away from those around us in an attempt to somehow protect ourselves.

When you hide your uniqueness and your strengths, you separate yourself from the truth: that you really are awesome and limitless. When you embrace your qualities and uniqueness, then you will truly own your personal power, and as a result, begin to live a life that has true meaning for you. When your uniqueness goes unexpressed in the world, the spark that makes you a one-of-a-kind individual never has the chance to become the flame it needs to be. It is important to be aware that as you begin to recognize and own your qualities, these three roadblocks can hinder the process:

▶▶ You may deny and minimize how unique and special your qualities are.

▶▶ You only recognize and value the qualities that are valued by others, and

▶▶ You may resist your new awareness out of fear of having a 'big ego'.

Exercise: Owning Your Qualities

The purpose of this exercise is to help you focusing on who you are rather than what you do. Owning and embracing what makes you unique allows your Being and Doing sides to work together. Stress is reduced and you can begin to enjoy life more easily.

Step 1 (a)   Look at the Qualities list following these exercise directions. Check off every quality that is part of you. Some may be easily recognized by you – others you may not have seen in a while. Do not censor or judge yourself – simply have fun checking them off!

Step 1 (b)   When working with the list, notice how you feel. Notice your brain chatter. Are you trying to deny that you have a certain amazing quality? Are you trying to minimize that it is actively present in your daily life? Example: women often deny that they are creative because they are not good at crafts. Think about everything you need to do, create and orchestrate to get through each and every day. This is pure creation at its best!

_____

_____

_____

_____

_____

_____

Step 2)   Once you feel satisfied that you have checked them all off and have added any others, it is time to develop your Top 10 List. In the space to the right of the Qualities list, write the numbers 1 through 10 in a column. You do not need to place them in any particular order, but choose your Top 10 qualities.

Suggestion: Focus on choosing the top 10 qualities that YOU define yourself as having, not what others say that you have. Do this for yourself, as you are owning and healing that rift in yourself. You are becoming stronger and more aware of your uniqueness. Really value what you find, knowing that some people around you may not value that quality as much as others. Example: We are living in a society where being extroverted (expressing yourself easily and living large) is highly valued. Qualities such as being gentle, peaceful and patient may not seem to be very valuable – yet they are! These qualities provide the strong foundation on which a balanced life is built. Embrace the value in them for yourself.

Write your Top 10 Qualities (in no particular order) here:

1) _____

2) _____

3) _____

4) _____

5) _____

6) _____

7) _____

8) _____

9) _____

10) _____

Step 3)   From the list of 10, choose your top three qualities - the ones that you value most in yourself. Write them down below the Top 10 list, again in no particular order.

1) _____

2) _____

3) _____

If you have found this exercise challenging, you are not alone. As women, we are taught from an early age 'not to blow our own horn'. This belief no longer works in today's fast-paced world where our inner light needs to shine each and every day. Stress will be reduced and your inner strength with blossom!

Step 4)   Write this Top Three list down and take it with you in your daily life. Look at them throughout the day and reflect on their importance. Begin to recognize when these qualities appear during the day. Focus on your strengths, and what you consider to be 'weaknesses' will not dominate your thoughts or your view of yourself.

Owning Your Qualities

- ❑ Affectionate
- ❑ Appreciative
- ❑ Artistic
- ❑ Assertive
- ❑ Brave
- ❑ Business-like
- ❑ Calm
- ❑ Caring
- ❑ Committed
- ❑ Common sense
- ❑ Communicator
- ❑ Compassionate
- ❑ Considerate
- ❑ Contented
- ❑ Cooperative
- ❑ Creative
- ❑ Curious
- ❑ Dedicated
- ❑ Dependable
- ❑ Diligent
- ❑ Disciplined
- ❑ Eager
- ❑ Efficient
- ❑ Encouraging
- ❑ Excited about life
- ❑ Fair
- ❑ Feeling

- ❑ Focused
- ❑ Forceful
- ❑ Forgiving
- ❑ Frank
- ❑ Free-spirited
- ❑ Friendly
- ❑ Funny
- ❑ Generous
- ❑ Gentle
- ❑ Happy
- ❑ Hard working
- ❑ Health conscious
- ❑ Honest
- ❑ Humorous
- ❑ Imaginative
- ❑ Independent
- ❑ Inspiring
- ❑ Intelligent
- ❑ Joyful
- ❑ Leader
- ❑ Listens well
- ❑ Logical
- ❑ Lovable
- ❑ Loving
- ❑ Loyal
- ❑ Motivating
- ❑ Musical

- ❑ Non-judgmental
- ❑ Observant
- ❑ Orderly
- ❑ Open
- ❑ Patient
- ❑ Peaceful
- ❑ Perservering
- ❑ Pleasant
- ❑ Positive
- ❑ Protective
- ❑ Quick learner
- ❑ Resilient
- ❑ Respectful
- ❑ Responsible
- ❑ Risk taking
- ❑ Sensual
- ❑ Sensitive
- ❑ Spiritual
- ❑ Spontaneous
- ❑ Straight forward
- ❑ Strong
- ❑ Team player
- ❑ Tolerant
- ❑ Trusting
- ❑ Understanding
- ❑ Visionary
- ❑ Wise

Add any other that is not on this list:

_____

_____

Cherish forever what makes you unique 'cuz you're really
a yawn if it goes.

-Bette Midler, entertainer.

Chapter 2

Redefining Success for Women

**Our new definition of success takes our
whole lives into consideration.**

In part, success is how well we accomplish what we set out to
attain. It is about our goals meeting our dreams, and the thrill of
exceeding what we had expected. Success is about thriving and
flourishing personally and financially. Yet, we are beginning to learn
that success is not solely the destination. It is also about our daily life
and how we live it. With regard to defining success in our lives, we are
beginning to take our 'whole lives' into consideration.

The bottom line is that women are hungry for a new definition
of success. A new approach that flows from the core of who we are based
on our needs and desires, those of our family and the requirements of our
work and our dreams. At the core of this are our own needs and desires.
Understand that the foundation for living a balanced, less-stressed life is
found in shifting your perspective to yourself. Redefining success for
women - and especially for yourself - provides you with a new
foundation from which to live your life.

> This is a new foundation through which you can thrive, and not merely survive, all the things that you need to accomplish and complete in a day.

Through redefining what success means for you in your life, you will:

▸▸ Have a new roadmap for success.

▸▸ Experience a greater focus in thinking.

▸▸ Find greater meaning and satisfaction in all your daily work.

▸▸ Choose how you will use your energy.

▸▸ Bust stress and easily increase self-care.

▸▸ Really own that you are an awesome and limitless woman!

The Meaning of Success

Let's look at what success means in a way that fits for women's lives and provides a new value system from which to live and attain your goals. What does success really mean to you? Is it about more life balance and less stress? Is it about paying the bills and making ends meet? Is it about acquiring the finer things in life? Is it about the next promotion, or the expansion of a current business? Is it about feeling healthier and more contented in life? Is it all of the above? There is no right or wrong way in regards to what success means to you. You are a multi-faceted woman and you desire and strive for many forms of success in your life. Yet, the way you are striving for it in our lives now simply wears you out!

Success means different things to different people. For women, it also means different things based on the age and stage we are at in our lives. For a woman who is a student or starting her career, it is different than for a woman with children or teens at home. And, for a woman whose children are leaving the nest, or a woman who is aging and may have increased demands from her parents, success has a different meaning. Yet, regardless of the age of a woman or the stage in her life, there is a common inner conflict in regards to success.

> What increases our stress is that our internal belief system for what success means comes from an outdated source that is based on the values of others and not ourselves.

This outdated view has these values at its core:

▶▶ Thinking of success as something in the future, and not in the here and now.

▶▶ Seeing success through how others have defined it.

▶▶ Seeing ourselves as successful only when someone says or validates that we are.

What if you began to see yourself as a success in whatever you are doing today? What if you started seeing yourself as a successful woman based upon your unique qualities, and how you express them each day? What if you see your success in every problem you solve, every task you do, every smile you give, and with every nose you wipe?

> Being able to value who you are and all that you do as success catapults your energy to new levels. It allows you to hold your own importance in the midst of all that is usually defined as insignificant.

So, how have we learned to undervalue so much of what we do that expresses our true nature and reflects our uniqueness? It is an outcome of both gender's beliefs about success, and how this belief system is active at home, at work, in business, and within most of the contacts that we have each day. As women, we have learned to internalize these beliefs and make them part of how we define ourselves. In addition, our internal turmoil is heightened as these outdated beliefs about success conflict with our true nature and what success really means to us.

The Root of Our Beliefs

Knowing the source of our beliefs about success is critical as we use, expend and replenish our personal energy based upon these core beliefs.

Our Beliefs about Success

Women's work has been greatly undervalued.

Women believe this and undervalue themselves.
This impacts our

Self-esteem   Motivation   Self-Care   Creativity

Focus   Goal Attainment   Desires

These beliefs about being successful are rooted in the lives and the teachings of our mothers and grandmothers, and the countless generations before them. They lived very different lives than we do today. Most of them lived their lives defining who they were through their husbands and families. Their roles were clearly defined, the expectations for how they were 'supposed to' live were clear, and these roles were not challenged. There was very little recognition of their own dreams and desires. Actually, for a woman to follow her dreams apart from family life, or take on different roles for herself required a great deal of courage. She often felt like and 'outsider', and was treated this way by both men and women.

So, we as women in the 21st Century learned how to use our energy, to respond to others, and to even 'follow the rules' by what the women before us had learned to believe about themselves. This is not about blaming them for the challenges we face today. There is no way that they could have prepared us for what we need to know today. At the core of the work that women before us did was the belief that their work really did not have any value. No matter how hard they worked to establish their homes, farms, or family businesses, their contributions were never really acknowledged. Their work was not given a monetary value nor recognized as being the foundation of the survival and growth of the family and their communities.

This is critical for us as we still carry this belief about the value of our work with us. You may not think that you do, yet we all do to some extent. Are you a woman who works outside the home, yet still does the majority of work at home? Are you a woman who works in your home caring, for your family on a full-time basis and thinks that your work is not as important as a woman with a paid career? Just for today, tune in to your belief about the value of your work and you'll begin to notice how you undervalue what you do throughout your day. This belief needs to change. As long as you believe that your work (whatever it is) does not have value, then you are only hurting yourself – draining your energy, eroding your esteem and sabotaging your success.

The Outdated 20th Century Model of Success

We will begin this process of helping you define success for you by first understanding the 20th century definition of success. It is outdated, yet still the basis of how we see success in our lives.

> Traditionally, success has been defined as attaining a goal that has been given a value.

This seems straightforward enough. But, for how you approach work as a woman, there are two difficulties with this definition:

> We have learned to define ourselves as successful only when we attain a goal.

This means that the road that we take and the process of achieving the goal are not seen as important. (The conflict for us is that the journey we take to reach our goals is very important with regard to how we work towards attaining a goal.) The second problem with this definition today is:

> We allow other people – not us – to determine the value of the goal .

If others - whether co-workers, family members or friends - see what we work for and achieve as being valuable, then we see ourselves as attaining something worthwhile. We believe to value what we achieve through how other people see us. And when we take this personally, we value ourselves through how other see us as well.

So we have learned to believe that we are only successful when we have actually achieve something that someone else sees or judges as being valuable. It is important to know this as we carry this kind of belief deep within our core. How you see yourself, how you take care of yourself, and how you work each day flows from this belief, whether you are aware of it or not. Have you ever felt empty working towards a goal or after an accomplishment? If yes, look back on it, and ask yourself how much of the value of what you were working towards was determined by others and not owned by yourself?

Here we are as women working hard to fulfill our dreams and attain our goals while working out of an old value system about success that does not really work for us, and is outdated all together. Think about how rapidly our roles have changed over the past 30 years. As a result, you have had few role models to guide the way. It also demonstrates the amount of courage it takes us to make the changes you are making to live your life in this new way.

The Outdated 20th Century Model of Success

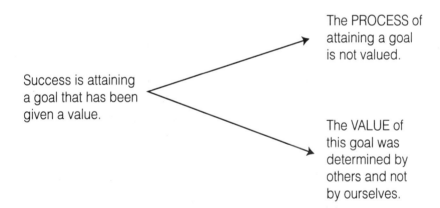

This outdated model:

- ▶▶ Does not affirm you and all that you do each and every day.

- ▶▶ Does not let you know that you are deserving of success.

- ▶▶ Does not include recharging your batteries.

- Does not leave room for you to have needs, nor to get them met.

- Does not give you permission to enjoy who you meet nor what you do along the way.

The New Model of Success for Women

Today, success for women is about the *process of reaching and attaining a particular goal*. For us as women, the path we take to attain our goals can be more important to us than the actual goal we are trying to attain. We want to fully experience the ride while getting to the destination. Looking at success this way allows us to revel in each day and work in a way that has value and meaning for us. Recall too that with the old definition of success, the value of the goal is how others define it. If others saw you as successful, then you were.

> Imagine how much stress you will end by seeing yourself as successful each day. Imagine how empowering it will be to begin to notice the small accomplishments you attain each day, and to know that each small step is a success.

With this new definition of success for you as a woman, know that:

- Others may influence the value of this goal, but your power is how you determine and define the goal for yourself.

- Recognizing and enjoying the success you have in your life now is the key to feeling fulfilled.

- The experience of the journey on the road we take to attain our goals can be as, or even more, important to us than actually reaching our destination.

At this point, you may be wondering:

> 'How do I learn to have a more inner
> focus, with goals defined by myself?
> How do I begin to notice my
> successes on a daily basis when my
> life seems to be so determined by
> other people?'

This is such a common question for women, but one that is rarely addressed by goal-setting programs. This book is about helping you learn how to do this — to learn to work and accomplish your goals in a way that reduces your stress, and lets you feel that your life has more meaning for you!

Blocks to Believing that We are a Success

Let's look at two beliefs that women may carry in their lives that can block this shift from easily occurring. Remember that beliefs are deep-rooted, internal values. These core beliefs affect how you live your life, use your energy, and how quickly you attain your goals. And, what is critical is that you may not even be aware of them!

Blocking Belief #1 - The Fear of Being Self-Centered: The first belief that blocks the door to success is about our conflict as women in having a self-centered focus in life. As women, we began learning at an early age that we need to put the concerns, needs, goals, desires and dreams of others before our own. Some women get this message more strongly than others, but it has been a part of how we have been socialized. The remedy to this is developing a 'healthy selfishness' through building a stronger relationship with yourself, and letting *you* be the focal point of your life.

One of the greatest fears that we have in moving from an outer or 'other' focus to a self or stronger 'me' focus is that we will become and remain selfish. Do you ever find that at every party there is that one person who can corner you and talk about no one but him/herself and their life? This person has no real interest in you or your life - they only want an audience. Our fear, as women, in moving to 'healthy selfishness' is that we will swing like a pendulum, and become that person. Don't worry, this will not happen! In the next chapter, there are tips and tools to help you develop healthy selfishness. Some of the personal and professional benefits to doing this are:

- ▶▶ Beginning to live life in away that has meaning for you.

- ▶▶ Finding that you become more focused, and productive.

- ▶▶ Giving stress less control in your life.

- ▶▶ Starting to feel more in charge of your life.

- ▶▶ Making better choices in how you work and use your energy, and

- ▶▶ Turning on the 'success magnet' that is already inside of you.

Blocking Belief #2 - Needing to Be in Control: The second inner belief that women have which blocks success and leaves us overworked is our belief about being in control. We think that being 'in control' means that our lives will be more organized, less stressful and more productive. Actually hidden in the word 'control' is the need to be controlling of others and ourselves. Here is an example: *'If I need to be in control in my life that means that it has to be ordered and perfect. In order for me to be in control of my life, then I need to be ordered and perfect all of the time as well.'* This becomes the driving force for your energy.

As women, we forget that we are human beings and not human doings. And when we believe that our lives need to be ordered and perfect all of the time, we are living life based in the fear of not being in control. This is incredibly self-defeating! We expend so much energy and time by trying to control others and ourselves that we are not able to smoothly attain our goals. We worry about things that really are not important and often waste our energy. What being in control does is put up a huge roadblock to our success and, actually, keeps us spinning our wheels in the same spot! What it also does is keep you disconnected from the two greatest tools you have to achieve success and live a life that has meaning for you — your intuition and your creativity.

The goal is not to live life in control, but rather live life in charge.

> Living in charge means that you can clearly determine your path to success based on your dreams and needs, while letting go of the ways of living and working that have actually increased the stress in your life and created roadblocks to your success.

So, now you can see that the two main internal belief blocks to success that women have are 1) not living life based in 'healthy selfishness', and 2) being in charge really means needing to be in control of others and ourselves. Next, let's move to an empowering definition of success that can help you see your work and your life in a new way.

The Empowering Definition of Success

Success is based on a woman's needs, dreams and desires

↓

The value of the goal may be influenced
by others, but Determined by Herself

↓

Success is seen as both
the *journey* of reaching and
actual *attainment* of a goal.

Whether you are working full-time as a caregiver, in business for yourself, or employed by a company, you can use this definition in your approach to your work and your life. If you do, two things begin to change. First, you actually feel more satisfied and fulfilled on a daily basis. Second, you are committing to living life with success in mind.

Don't just work, but also play with your new definition of success. Playing includes looking at success in a light-hearted way. Through this, creativity can flow and your true limitless nature will rapidly unfold. Avoid creating more stress in your life by making career and life choices that are in conflict with your new definition of success. (See exercise at the end of this chapter). Review, revise and recharge your definition of success today, and start really enjoying all your successes in the here and now.

Success Tips for the 21st Century Woman

To help you with redefining success and focusing on your goals in a new way, here are four proven strategies that keep you on track:

▶▶ Decision-making

▶▶ Energetically shifting a problem

▶▶ Using the power of intention

▶▶ Persevering, persevering, persevering

Success Tip #1 – Decision-making

Women are phenomenal at decision-making. If you are shaking your head in disagreement with this statement, you are not alone. That's because you may often feel like you get through the day with a cloud of confusion over your head, and feeling like you are not really accomplishing much.

The key is in knowing that you are continually making decisions throughout the day, yet not recognizing that you are making them. You may also not recognize the sheer number that you make. Women tend to focus on the problems that won't seem to go away rather than the dozens of things that they've accomplished. (Again, this goes back to the outdated belief that our work really is not that important, so therefore the decisions that we make are not valuable either). Begin turning this around by simply noticing the decisions that you do make, and give yourself credit for all you accomplish.

Would you like some help for those problems that never seem to go away? We can become anxious and immobilized by going over and over issues in our thoughts – especially those involving other people. We become stuck as an outcome of our fear. We are anxious and worried that we will not make the right decision, disappoint someone or seem selfish. The solution to this starts by beginning to give your fear away. When you find that you are agonizing over a decision, you need to call in your greatest ally to help. This ally is known as your *'highest self'*.

This 'highest self' is the source of your greatest inner wisdom. This reservoir of wisdom and insight is blocked when you are stuck in fear-based thinking. You'll learn much more about your 'highest self' and how to access her in your daily life through the process of working with this book. For now, when you are stuck making a decision, ask yourself this question:

What would a wise woman advise me to do now?

By asking this, you will open the door to your inner wisdom and tap into some phenomenal energy and direction. You really do have all the answers for your life within yourself. This process is about asking the right question, listening to the answer and beginning to trust yourself on a deeper level. Approaching decision-making this way will let the process begin.

Success Tip #2 – Energetically Shifting a Problem

We've looked at how decision-making is hampered by fear. When you ask our 'highest self' for assistance, you choose to take a new look at the issue at hand. This energetically shifts a problem. It takes the focus and the power away from the block, and puts the energy towards the solution. There are a couple of additional approaches that you can use to energetically shift a problem. Your intention is to release any and all stress associated with it. Fear is the number one stress, but other stressors appear in other forms.

One stressor is our self-defeating thinking, which we will look at and learn to undo at depth in a later chapter. Self-defeating thinking is any thought or thought process that puts you or others down. It may be a direct thought about your inability to do something, or it may even be through not giving yourself credit for the talents and skills that you have. Reversing this is an incredibly powerful experience and will really accelerate your ability to attain your goals.

> Put your energy, thoughts, intent
> and beliefs into finding the solution
> rather than focusing on the block.

We often get bogged down by the process of indecision. We forget that if we believe that we have the solution we will reach it so much more quickly. Focus on the fact that you are working in 'real time' – that your focus is on the present. We become energetically stuck by focusing on issues from the past or worrying about the future. Neither the past nor future are real, so focus your energy and intent on the here-and-now.

Success Tip #3 – The Power of Intention

Intention is about having a focused purpose. It is knowing where you want to go and having an idea about how to get there. It is about staying focused and goal-oriented. The power of intention is about uplifting yourself and others. It is fueled by working with your 'highest self and highest good' for whatever issue or problem that is at hand.

What blocks us from attaining our goals as women is not so much the day to day challenges in our lives, but rather that we get pulled away from our intended purpose. We allow others to use too much of our time or energy, or we second-guess ourselves and what we desire to attain. We may even sabotage ourselves through our thoughts and actions. Whatever way – or ways – that we are doing this we are giving permission to ourselves and others to take our goals away from us.

Knowing the reality of our lives, this will happen. How many times have you started a day with a list of things to do that were important to you and, by the end of the day, none of them had occurred? How often have the urgent needs and demands of the people in your life pulled you away from what you wanted to accomplish? The key is not to get discouraged and give up on yourself. This is critical, because when you do, you give away the power of your intention. Discouragement is like a very bad computer virus. Its damage occurs when you are not looking, and by the time that you discover it, so much damage has already been done. Become very aware of your thoughts and actions so that you do not turn your frustration in on yourself.

> **When you trust and believe that you will attain your goals — even in the face of adversity and demands from others — then you will!**

If you allow your intention to waiver, the energy created from this will undermine whatever you are trying to attain. When our intention and conviction are strong, and we become sidetracked, it will only be temporary. Connect with a supportive network of other women who know and understand your goals, and who will hold them up for you, even when you have forgotten them. This will reinforce your ability to stay on track in the midst of life demands.

Success Tip #4 – Persevere, Persevere, Persevere

Women are experts at perseverance. Since the beginning of time, we have known how to continually put one foot in front of the other to get the needs of our families met. We have been able to do this regardless of the crises at hand, the limited resources we may have, the endless challenges in our lives, and through the repetitive nature of our daily work. We have done this with grit, determination, and know-how to push through obstacles without wavering.

We have always been able to do this for others. We have not been as great at doing this for ourselves. One of the reasons is that we have not had a lot of practice! Recall how significantly our lives have changed from those of our mother's and grandmother's. It is only now that we can focus on our needs and desires, and not live our lives based on the needs of others.

If you find that you have never lived your life based on 'you', then you are not alone. This really is new to women. Here are some pointers that will help:

Give yourself permission to persevere on your own behalf.

Refuse to feel the fear that you will somehow lose if you take a stand for yourself.

Use what you are instinctually able to do for others' and do it for yourself.

Keep your goals in the forefront of your life.

Stop judging whether your goals are really are important or not.

Your goals and perseverance are the key to manifesting what you desire.

So, you may be wondering, *'where do I go from here?'* The following step-by-step exercise will help you to develop a definition of success that works for you, and fits with your life today. Any change is a process, so know that what you come up with today is not carved in stone. It will change and grow as you do.

Exercise: Boosting Your Focus on Success

1)   Through reading this chapter, what did you uncover about your
        current beliefs about success *for you?*

        _____

        _____

        _____

        _____

        _____

        _____

2)   Ask yourself: 'With all I have learned in life, what part of these
        beliefs still fit for me in my life? What part of these beliefs no
        longer fit?'

        _____

        _____

        _____

        _____

        _____

        _____

3)   Ask yourself: 'How does holding onto what doesn't fit impact
        upon my life? How do these beliefs block my success today,
        and my ability to recognize when I am successful?'

        _____

        _____

_____

_____

_____

_____

4)   Ask yourself: 'How do I envision (a) success in my life at work (whatever my work may be), and (b) in my life? Which elements of these do I need to include in a new definition of success for me?'

_____

_____

_____

_____

_____

5)   Write for yourself a new definition of success that will provide you with a mission statement for your life.
Success for me means:

_____

_____

_____

_____

_____

_____

Success is, for the most part, not just an accident or a matter of blind "luck", but a result of having a clear picture for the future.

- Faith Popcorn, from 'Clicking'

Chapter 3

Energy Choicing in Daily Life

Energy Choicing is the cornerstone for being in charge in our lives.

These two words - energy and choice - both carry a particular 'charge' for us. We often react to the word 'energy' as we never seem to have enough of it, yet feel our work is always demanding more. When we hear the word 'choice' – as a woman – our immediate thoughts are often *'Choice, what choice do I have in my life?'* Learning to think of energy and how you choose it in a new way will change your life. There are not many guarantees in life, yet this is one!

If we define energy from a purely scientific perspective we will have a technical definition – but this is not how we (as women) really understand and experience our energy in our daily lives. The way we have learned to define energy is a limited one, and often think of energy as something that we do not have enough of! How often do you think to yourself how tired you are through the day, or question if the demands are ever going to end? How often do you wish you had more energy? Well, you are not alone. Most women are experiencing this today.

When we feel energized, we can tackle the world, take on lots of different roles and even feel inspired and creative. When we have a lack of energy we can feel exhausted, angry, repressed and even fearful. The interesting thing is that, as women, we often feel like we live in one of these two extremes. Either we feel like a supercharged dynamo or have the energy of a couch potato. We rarely experience the place between the two: the place of greater balance where the amount of energy that we output fits with how our energy gets replenished.

The Energy Pendulum

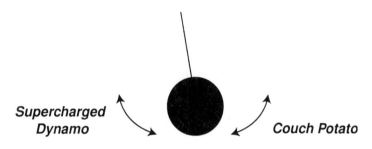

**We tend to live our lives swinging
between two energetic opposites.**

   The reality of our lives is that we are busy and have so many demands on our time, focus, and energy. If I were to say that there is a way to totally feel balanced in your life and have tons of energy all the time, I would be lying to you. Yet there are proven, effective ways of taking the load of your shoulders and to move through life and all the challenges of your day with less effort and without losing who you are in the process. Knowing what our energy really is all about will help begin this transition.

Energy Flow
   Energy is often defined solely by the amount of pep or stamina that we have. Do you ever find yourself focusing on not having enough energy and trying to find ways to 'get' more? Yet we need to understand what our energy is all about, and to learn how to use our energy more effectively in order to transform our lives and attain our goals. There is another way to look at our energy as well!

The essence of understanding about energy is the flow of it that continually moves through your body. You have energy pathways in your body, and the force that feeds and nurtures your physical self flows through them. These pathways are invisible to the naked eye, yet are essential for your well-being and ongoing health. When these energy pathways are blocked or weak, your energetic self is not well fed. Know too, that your ability to focus and to recognize the synchronicities in life that often leads to success is guided by this life force flow of energy.

Blocks in this flow of energy lead to increased fatigue, lowers the immune system, impacts mental health, and reduces the ability to focus and persevere. Blocks in this energy flow occur in so many ways, and stress is one of the main contributors to the block in its flow. For us as women, the stress that is created in our lives through how we have learned to live each and every day, and the pressures that we place on ourselves (and allow others to do) so greatly impacts the healthy flow of energy in our bodies. You may find that your energy is changing simply reading this. Know that understanding this energy and removing the blocks to this flow is new learning for all of us. Know too that the concepts, direction and exercises in this book will help greatly in the lessening of these energy blocks.

The F.A.S.T. Model for Understanding Energy

Understanding and opening our energy in this new way actually provides the flow needed to see your success now, and to have more energy and focus in attaining your goals.

F Fuel – how you charge and recharge your battery.

A Attitude – how you view your life, your relationships and your challenges.

S Self – how well you know yourself, recognize your needs, and determine your goals.

T Triad of all three

Fuel – Fuel means the actual calories you put in your body as well as the quality of the food you eat. It also means learning which foods are optimal to eat based on any sensitivities and even your body type. Fuel also refers to how you charge and recharge your body on a daily basis, including regular physical, mental and spiritual practices that strengthens your body and feeds your soul. (Refer to Chapter 4 on Self-Care.)

Attitude – Perception is everything. Your thoughts can increase or decrease your self-esteem, inner peace, the quality of your relationships, your view of success in your life today, and the attainment of your future goals. Attitude greatly impacts on whether you see life challenges as insurmountable problems or conduits for life learning. (Refer to Chapter 5 on Self-Defeating Thinking.)

Self – The relationship that you have with yourself is the most important relationship in your life. We are living in a time where we now have permission to discover and uncover who we really are, yet the way we are living day-to-day does not necessarily support this.

Look around you. Aren't more women you know exploring who they really are, and including more things in their lives that feed their true nature? We are in the midst of incredible transformation where the belief that we are deserving is becoming part of our core belief about ourselves. We are discovering the awesome power available to us through connecting very deeply with ourselves and knowing more clearly what we need and, in turn, including this information in determining our life goals.

Triad - The triad of all three of these components – fuel, attitude and relationship with self – provide you with a deeper understanding what your energy really means. It also provides a roadmap increasing pep and stamina and enabling the flow of life force energy in your body to maintain health, focus and the sense of well-being.

What is Energy Choicing?

Recall the changes that have occurred in our work and home lives over the past 30 years. Based upon these changes, how we use our energy needs to change as well. The bottom-line is that we are not making great choices about how we are using our energy and the decisions that we are making at work and home. If you are a woman who makes you career in the home with your family, the way that you use energy needs to be based on your choices rather than solely on the demands of others.

Let's look at the way that we have learned to expend our energy in our lives. (And 'expend' is a great word to use to describe what we do as we tend to give, and give, and give throughout the day.) We often use the same amount of energy for whatever the task or request is made of us. By doing this we keep disconnected from our goals and ourselves.

About using and giving our energy, we learned that it first goes to our immediate family — this means anyone who lives in our home with us who we consider family members. Secondly, it goes to extended family, which includes any blood relation you have a relationship with and feel connection. (Think of your cousin who calls you two days before you move, and even though you say you have other plans, you somehow drop it all and include this in your day). Thirdly, our energy goes to our work and career demands and goals. Now two (extended family) and three (work) are often interchangeable. Fourthly, our energy goes to our community, which can include our work, children's school, church activities, volunteer work and fundraising. The remainder of our energy goes to all others, which could include neighbors or people you barely know. And where is a woman in this model. Dead last! And 'dead' is the operative word, as women feel energetically dead giving all to others and having some for herself if there is any left.

The Traditional Use of Our Energy

Energy Goes to:

Extended Family

Work

Community

Others

Self

Notice how small the word 'Self' is. The outcome of how we chronically expend our energy now, we become this small – and at times invisible – in our own lives.

So the current way that we expend our energy:

- ▶▶ Doesn't affirm us as people with needs.
- ▶▶ Minimizes recharging our batteries.
- ▶▶ Smothers our inner flame and spark.
- ▶▶ Turns off our ability to be 'success magnets'.
- ▶▶ Allows us to forget that we are worthy and deserving.
- ▶▶ Blocks us in attaining our goals and enjoy successes.
- ▶▶ Doesn't give us the room to recognize and express our needs.
- ▶▶ Eradicates any space for healthy, supportive relationships.

The New Approach – Energy Choicing

'Energy Choicing' is the new, take-charge approach to using energy that opens the door to a less exhausted future for women! Through learning Energy Choicing strategies, you give yourself the tools and permission to use your energy in a new way that keeps you at the center in your life. Choosing the amount of energy that you use for any particular task, job, and activity or even in a crisis is what Energy Choicing is all about. And choosing how you use your energy is the key to stopping the swing between the extremes of the supercharged dynamo or the exhausted couch potato.

In this new model you are is at the top and no longer at the bottom in your own life. You know that your energy is yours - and know that you have choices about how to use your energy. Check in with yourself. Are you feeling like this could not work or that it could be only a dream in your life? You are not alone in this feeling. For most women, when they begin looking at their energy and their life choices in a new way, some anxiety, fear or doubt may arise as a result of the old belief system you still have inside. This will shift when you begin to approach how you use your energy in a different way, and begin to understand that it can be done differently. Your body learns that:

1) You do not need to give your energy to just anyone that demands it,

2) You no longer need to use the same amount of energy for every task,

3) You have ways to recharge your battery and feel more energized, and

4) You are in charge in your life.

Typically, a woman gives first to her immediate family and then her chosen family. Your immediate family members are those people who live or have lived under the same roof as you with whom you have a significant relationship. This enables you to create the foundation on which to anchor your life. What is really different about this new model of how a woman uses her energy is that of having *chosen family* members. They are the people that you may or may not be related to by blood, and they are the people to whom you are the personally closest to in life.

> **Chosen family members are the people who support you, inspire you and nurture you in a way that has real meaning for you in life. Using your energy to be connected with, or to help them, does not seem like such a burden, and you get a great deal back through your relationships with them.**

The third part of this new model is the role of work and career. As you see, it comes after immediate and chosen family members. Energy goes to extended family members, then to the community, and then to all others. With this approach, you choose how much energy you give to each person and task. The foundation for this new approach is that you come first, and that you have the ultimate choice and decision making about how your energy is used, and where you put it for your highest good and the highest good of the people who have the most priority in your life. Know too that in the 'real world', there will be times when this approach is not as clear, and you feel like you come last again. The goal is to have your life working this way most of the time — where you are choosing how to use your energy, and that you come first, not last.

> **Energy choicing is about knowing that you always have choice about how much energy you will spend on a task, and about making choices that are optimal for you.**

When you follow this model, you will experience some real changes in your attitude towards yourself. These changes will improve how smoothly you attain your goals and you will find that you will have more fun along the way! One change is that you will find yourself on top in your own life, and feeling more confident about the fact that you have choices, and about the choices you make. A second change is that you will find you will be receiving more from others, and there will be a greater balance between giving and receiving. You'll have a greater experience of the joy of loving others and feeling loved yourself. You will also find that you feel more deserving of success and your accomplishments, and you will feel more fulfilled in your life. Stress will have less control in your life, feelings of guilt will reduce, and you will be able to state what you need and desire.

Any real change is a process, so know that you will notice these changes over time with unbelievable results. When you strategically use your energy and put yourself first-not-last, your 'success magnet' becomes stronger, and you actually feel less stress in your life.

The New Approach – Energy Choicing

Tools for Energy Choicing

> Energy Choicing keeps you on the fast track to attaining your goals and living the balanced life that you deserve.

Energy Choicing is first about believing that you have a choice of how much energy you use. Often in our busy, stressed lives, we forget that we have a choice, and choosing is the cornerstone of being in charge in our own lives. We often use the same amount of energy for whatever we tackle - whether it is an important job or a minor one in our lives. We want to give 100 % all of the time. We don't realize that doing this leads to exhaustion, frustration and actually slows down our progress in attaining our goals.

Remember this as you approach the next few tasks or challenges in your life, and know that you have the choice about the amount of energy that you expend in doing each task, solving a problem, or dealing with a particular person. Know too that the flip side of this is that you will have an energy reserve available to tackle the really important issues, or to give someone in your life that 100% that they may need. The five questions for smarter choices are:

1) **'How much of a priority is this task?'**

   Tip: When prioritizing, I look at the importance of the task in the grand scheme of life. The question that keeps me on track is "Will this change the course of the Universe?" If the answer is no – and it always is – I find that my anxiety is reduced and I look at the task from a rational rather than an emotional basis.

2) **'How much energy in thought or through action do I want to use with this particular situation?'**

   Tip: Remember that energy choicing is about taking the power of Choice and using it for yourself. As women, we tend to use the same amount of energy for every task, job, interaction, relationship and issue. The bottom-line is that we will have more energy if we choose how much we will give to each of these things.

3) **'How much energy have I used on a similar problem in the past, and what did I learn that can help me now?'**

   Tip: Do you ever feel like you are doing the same things over and over again? I have never met a woman who says no! We have many solutions from solving past problems that we can use today. By denying that we have this knowledge, we are not owning our power and continue to 'spin our wheels'. Imagine having a big duffel bag that holds all your past solutions. Imagine reaching in to that bag to find the solution to your current problem. Trust the results.

4) **'How much resistance am I creating with regard to performing this task or dealing with this person?'**

   Tip: Start by admitting how you are truly feeling about the challenge or the task at hand. Do you find that something needs to be done that you do not really want to do? Do you find that you are doing something that really is not your responsibility, or your sole responsibility? This feeling of resistance can often be a gift. It can tell you that you are being overly responsible - one of the key pitfalls for women. Being overly responsible is about having too much ownership about what you are trying to accomplish and its outcome. This could mean that you are working or trying hard, feeling overly responsible for the task or situation, or expecting a perfect solution to a problem.

5. **'Am I responding or reacting to the challenge at hand?'**
    When stressed our internal 'fuse' can become quite short. As a result we often react in a knee-jerk, stress producing way to things such as the view of others, the reality of the situation, or even our own needs and desires. Ask yourself, 'Am I responding or reacting to this particular situation or person?'

    When you respond, you are in the energy choicing mode. You see the bigger picture and do not take things personally. Your thoughts are clear, and you are able to access and use all of you resources to find solutions. When you react, you may be trying to control and feeling fearful. As a result, your clarity in thinking and judgment is affected.

    Responding prevents and reduces stress.
    Reacting creates and increases stress!

Recap - Energy Choicing is about:

1) Knowing that you always have a choice about how much energy you will spend on a task.

2) Giving yourself permission to choose.

3) Following through and making choices that fit for you and the task or situation at hand.

Exercise: 5 Questions for Smarter Choices

These following questions will keep you focused on effective Energy Choicing. Think of a current challenge in your life that you are spending too much energy on. Answer each of the questions with the intention that you will find your truth in how you really want to use your energy.

1)   How much of a priority is this task?

_____

_____

_____

_____

_____

_____

2)   How much energy in thought or through action do I want to use with this particular situation?

_____

_____

_____

_____

_____

_____

3) How much energy have I used on a similar problem in the past, and what did I learn that can help me now?

_____

_____

_____

_____

_____

_____

4) How much resistance am I creating with regard to performing this task or dealing with this person?

_____

_____

_____

_____

_____

5)   Am I responding or reacting to the challenge at hand?

_____

_____

_____

_____

_____

_____

There is a vitality, a life force, a quickening that is translated through
you into action. There is only one of you in all time,
this expression is unique, and if you block it,
it will never exist through any other medium; and be lost.
                              - *Martha Graham, dancer and choreographer.*

Behold this day!
It is yours to make.

- Black Elk, Oglala Sioux mystic

Chapter 4

Stress and Self-Care in Women's Lives

Developing a self-care attitude turns on your 'success magnet'.

It is so easy for us as women to blame ourselves for the amount of stress in our lives. We easily fall in to believing that 'I'm not good enough' because 'I am not coping' with the challenges in my life. There is a belief that is very present and very contagious among us. This belief is that 'I must hold it all together' and appear as is I am coping beautifully, no matter what comes my way or however I feel. These beliefs no longer have purpose in our lives. Holding onto them stops us from pursuing our goals, living fully connected to ourselves, and having intimate, caring relationships.

The bottom-line is that there are too many demands on us and too much stress in our lives. There has really been a quickening in the speed of life, and there is no simple explanation for it. The reasons involve the nature of work, the complexity of the lives of our children, the changing needs of our family members, and the increased need in our communities to be volunteers to meet the gaps in services and simply to help.

Yet, the greatest, most powerful stressor in our lives comes from within. There is a pull from deep inside ourselves that comes from our soul. It's a voice that continually whispers – and sometimes shouts – that we are being lost in the process of our daily life demands. It is a pull that is trying to let us know that, as stress becomes more chronic and increases in our lives, that we are being pulled further and further away from our true nature and our real self. This division – between our functioning self each day and our real self inside – allows stress to be increased and magnified in our life. It also drains our energy. We need to unconsciously use energy to keep avoiding our inner truth and to continue to function in the way that we know, no longer works.

Stress and Success

Take a moment to reflect on the following statement: *Stress is Normal*. What is your immediate response – the first thing that pops into your head that you do not censor or judge? Is it any or all of the following:

➤ Yes I know it is normal, but is it ever going to end?

➤ How much 'normal' is a good thing?

➤ It can't be normal because it feels so horrible!

➤ If this is the way I have to keep living, then I'll just quit!

Most women have a real reaction to thinking of stress as being normal. You may have found that you chuckled and shook your head in disbelief, or became angry and anxious. There is no right or wrong answer or response. We are living in a time where our business and personal lives are moving at such a rapid pace that 'toxic stress' has become a real villain in our lives. The fact that non-toxic stress really does have a purpose has become lost. And as a result, we have learned to reject the *information* that the stress in our lives can be trying to provide for us.

A stress response is simply a biological response to a stimulus. Our bodies were built to respond to a situation that is perceived as being threatening, frightening or frustrating. Our adrenal glands 'kick-in' and get our bodies in gear to react to the stimulus. Dr. Hans Selye was the grandfather of stress research, and had linked the effects of stress to human illness and coined the term *'stress-general adaptation syndrome'*.* He found that stress is normal and that our body actually requires it to get us moving and to get the job done. What we have learned is that it is chronic and toxic stress that results in emotional, physical and spiritual imbalances.

> **Stress has gotten a 'bad reputation' because what we are actually experiencing today is chronic or toxic stress, and stress that is the result of rapid change.**

Toxic stress is a build-up of stress, often a result of so many 'little things' piling up on top of each other. We are dealing with so much stress that we often feel like we are like a hamster on a wheel — so caught up in the running that we forget how and when to jump off!

> **The bottom-line is that stress is here to stay. How you perceive it and deal with it can change. Serious Stress-Busting starts from within.**

* Dr. Hans Selye (1907-1982) was a Viennese-born physician who did most of his research on stress at McGill, and later, the University of Montreal. Through his research, he linked the effects of stress to human illness and coined the term 'stress-general adaptation syndrome'. In other words, he found that stress was normal and that our body actually requires it to get us moving.

The Stress Down Line

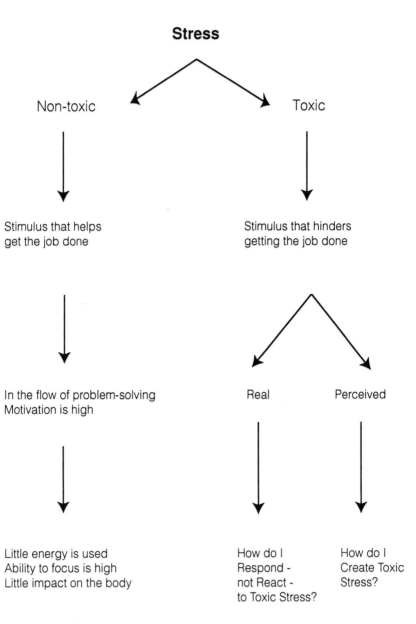

Stress

Non-toxic

Toxic

Stimulus that helps
get the job done

Stimulus that hinders
getting the job done

In the flow of problem-solving
Motivation is high

Real

Perceived

Little energy is used
Ability to focus is high
Little impact on the body

How do I
Respond -
not React -
to Toxic Stress?

How do I
Create Toxic
Stress?

Understanding the Stress Down-Line

The amount of stress in our lives is real, and the sources of it are as varied and unique as our lives. As we have learned, there is a certain amount of stress that we need and will remain a constant in women's lives. Know that no matter how effective we are at dealing with stress, there will be times of being overwhelmed and under-energized. If, these times are frequent, they can indicate that we have patterns of coping that do not work for us, or that there is something new that we need to learn. Yet, there is a key that will unlock the door that will provide relief at these times, and allow stress to escape. It is about learning how to *shift our perspective.*

But first, let's look at the chart which demonstrates the differences between non-toxic and toxic stress. On the left hand side of the chart, you can see that non-toxic stress helps us to get the job done. It is the type of stress that gives us the impetus to move forward, and complete a task or deal with an issue. Examples include a deadline at work, getting children to appointments, an interpersonal conflict that needs to be addressed, or the fact that the fridge is empty. We are in the flow of problem solving and our motivation is high. This type of stress has little 'wear and tear' on our bodies, and our ability to focus remains clear.

On the right hand side is toxic stress. If you are like many women today, the presence of toxic stress has become the normal way of living for you. Its greatest impact occurs when we are overwhelmed by the stress we are experiencing. Know that in these times of overload, it is very easy to 'make it worse' by thinking negatively and acting over - responsibly. In addition, it is much easier to be reactive rather than responsive to the tasks at hand, or the people with whom we are interacting.

It is critical for women to work with the information in this section, as well as seriously increase self-care. Think of it as wanting to be alive and healthy for the 'long-haul', and know that the challenges you are facing now in your life will not always be this awful for you. Trust this and take care of yourself.

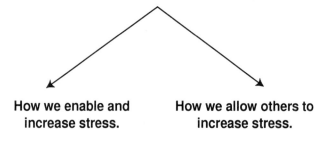

Keys to Decreasing the Stress That's Self-Created

How we enable and
increase stress.

How we allow others to
increase stress.

There are two ways that we can look at stress that will help you immediately reduce it in your life. The first begins with self, and is about how we enable it to increase and flourish in our lives. Again, this is not about self-blame, but is about understanding that there are times when we do it to ourselves, and it must stop. The second is through how we allow others to increase the stress in our lives, and, in turn, allow them and the stress to be in control of us.

Shifting Perspective

The key is understanding how our perceptions and attitudes effect stress. We can convert this non-toxic, motivating stress to toxic stress simply through the way that we perceive it. If I believe that stress will get to me or keep me down, then it will. If I believe that I cannot cope, then I won't. If I believe that there is no solution, then there will not be one. You'll learn in the section on self-defeating thinking that 'your body believes whatever your brain tells it'. Our body will react to whatever our thoughts are focused on. Simply ask yourself these questions when stressed:

How am I focusing on the negative?

How am I blaming myself for this stress and for how I feel?

These two questions will immediately shift your perspective, and will lead you to feel more in charge. The reason for this is that the minute you assess the stress, it no longer has control over you. It is almost as if you are looking at it from the outside-in, and seeing it for what it really is. This shift also allows you to let go of any stress that you are creating yourself.

Tunnel Vision

In shifting our perspective, we can look at how we tend to have 'Tunnel Vision' when stressed or in crisis. This means that we see the situation and other people involved through a very narrow range of vision. Tunnel Vision indicates to us that we have a fear response to whatever we are experiencing. What happens next is that alternatives and solutions are seen through a very narrow range as well. We are not able to see the big picture. Some signs of tunnel vision are:

- Frustration and confusion
- Black and white thinking (see self-defeating thinking patterns)
- Feeling trapped and alone
- Being closed to options or support from others
- Fatigue and lack of motivation
- Blocked creativity, intuition and problem-solving skills

It is important to be aware of the signs, because when experiencing tunnel vision, you are often not aware of it. When feeling trapped by stress, know that you are not looking at the options. The goal is simply to get out of the tunnel as quickly as you can! The following is an exercise to remove Tunnel Vision in a quick and easy manner.

Exercise: Eliminating Tunnel Vision

Sit at a desk or table with your elbows on the table. Lean over as if you are going to put your head in your hands. Instead, cup your hands around the sides of your eyes (as if you were a horse wearing blinders that keeps them from seeing from side to side). Keep your head bent forward and really connect with how this tunnel vision feels in your body. It will feel uncomfortable. Continue to do it until you get the sense of how it feels throughout your body. Remember to breathe deeply! Before you lift your head, read aloud the following intention with conviction:

"When I lift my head, the stress will lift and I'll leave the tunnel. I have a clear vision about what to do and will feel a sense of peace and calm."

Slowly lift your head, relax your hands and look around you. Breathe deeply and enjoy how less-stressed you feel.

Stress, Success and Self-Care

Through learning about Energy Choicing, you've already gained some strategic and powerful tools for reducing stress in your life. Next, you'll explore building a Self-Care Attitude, which forms a foundation for dealing with stress, recharging your battery and keeping your energy level high and your attitude positive. Again, this alters a woman's core beliefs about herself, which in turn creates a channel for success to flow. You also become a magnet attracting abundance into your life.

Self-care is based on desire. This desire is about improving how you treat yourself, reducing stress in your life, and strengthening your inner foundation.

> Self-care is anything positive that you do for yourself, which is solely for yourself, initiated by yourself and done because you desire it. It is about seeing and accepting that your

need for self-care is part of your humanness and that this human need is not the result of being deficient in some way.

Examples include setting time aside in the week solely for you, committing to regular activities in your life that you enjoy doing, getting away from all the demands of your life and doing what you would like — even for a few hours — or even having that regular massage appointment where you can relax and unwind. If your immediate reaction to this is that *'I don't have the time for this, nor the money'*, you are not alone. Many women have this initial reaction, but later find as they commit to their own self-care that the time frees up, and that they find approaches that cost little or no money.

Developing a self-care attitude is the key that unlocks the door to success. You may have some fear around listening to your desire and committing to self-care, because making it part of your life involves change. But once you acknowledge your desire for self-care, you can never go back. You may not listen to it at first, and may even try to bury it through self-defeating thoughts and self-denial; yet it will remain and continue to 'make noise' until you choose to listen.

The Four Levels of Self-Care

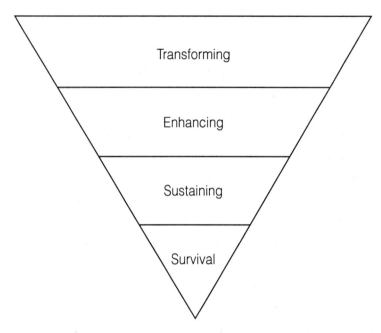

There are four levels of self-care for women that start at the survival level, and move up through sustaining, enhancing, and transforming self-care. As you evolve through the levels, a stronger foundation for living and success is created. Many women today are living at the level of survival self-care, with the experience of living at a sustaining level for short periods of time in their lives. It is critical that as you read this, you do not judge yourself for the quality or quantity of self-care in your life.

Developing a self-care attitude is a new approach for living. Again, the women before us did not really think this way about their lives. Look around you – how many women do you know who seem constantly 'stressed out', are unable to relax or sleep, and are prone to illness? All of these are signs that our bodies and spirits are unable to keep up with the demands of today the way we have been doing it.

> Building self-care into your
> foundation for living plays a huge
> role in transforming the life that you
> live to the life you desire.

Let's look more in depth at the progressive levels of self-care.

Level 1 - Survival Self-Care: These are the self-care actions that you take to simply survive when you are at the point of exhaustion in your life. It is those things you do that simply keep you going to the next moment or the next day. To recognize them, think of having an 'instant hit' of self-gratification. You may choose things that will elevate your mood and energy level immediately, and can often include food, alcohol or cigarettes – something that will change your mood instantly.

With the reality of our continually demanding lives, there is a role for survival self-care. Do not think that you need to get rid of it in your life. (By doing this, you will only cause another internal struggle, believing that you are having something taken away from you.) The key is to choose things that will instantly help that will not have a long-term detrimental effect on your health, mental wellness, or energy level. Coffee may stimulate you for a few moments, but the caffeine can create cravings later, or affect your sleep patterns and hormones. When you are in a moment when you feel that immediate need for gratification, ask yourself:

'How can I respond and not react to this need I am feeling?'

When we react, we tend to choose things that will not help us in the long run. When we respond, we still get our needs met in a new way that is healthier for us and will keep us on track with our overall game plan for our lives. Some suggestions for responding rather than reacting are to use:

- Essential oils and aromatherapy products (you can even keep these in your desk at work).
- *Bach Flower* remedies – especially Rescue Remedy (see your local health food store).
- *One-Minute Stress-Busting Skills* found later in this chapter.

The key is to reduce any survival self-care approaches that are detrimental to you, and use the ones that do not adversely affect you. As we are human, we will be impulsive about self-care at times. At those times, it is important not to 'beat yourself up' with your thinking as that will actually undo what you are trying to accomplish. As you increase your positive self-care, you will find that you will have less need for survival tactics that are really not helpful when looking at the bigger picture or your wellness.

Level 2 - Sustaining Self-Care: We have all experienced this next level of self-care. For some women, it has a regular place in their lives, yet for most it still does not. Often we decide that we are going to take better care of ourselves or include in our lives activities and healthy living approaches that feed us on many different levels. We do make that decision with the conviction and the desire that we are going to live lives for ourselves. We begin to enjoy this type of self-care, and feel an increase in our energy, and have a more positive attitude.

Unfortunately, this type of self-care is what we usually give away first when we go through those stressful times where the needs and demands of others begins to overwhelm us. We begin to leave out of our lives those activities and people who we have really begun to enjoy and feel good about. We focus on the problems at hand – usually created by others – and in turn abandon ourselves. Then, we wake up one day and realize that we are exhausted and sometimes feeling lost in our own lives (and often angry about this as well)! We revert to the survival mode of self-care.

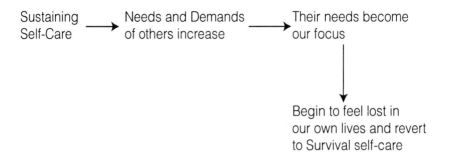

Sustaining Self-Care → Needs and Demands of others increase → Their needs become our focus

↓

Begin to feel lost in our own lives and revert to Survival self-care

The key is to be aware of this process as it occurs. If you want to be stronger, healthier and more successful in your life, you can no longer afford to give your enhancing self-care away.

Can I let you in on something? Sometimes, when others in our lives – often the people who live in our homes – see us becoming healthier, stronger and happier, they react to this. They see the shift in us and how we are changing. Many people, at their root, have a fear of change, and can create crises so that you will return to the way that you were – tired, unmotivated, and in survival mode – rather than have a 'new you' emerge. This may sound ridiculous, yet it is a pattern that frequently occurs and reoccurs in women's lives. Know that this could happen, and ride it out with your inner strength and resolve to take better care of yourself! What magically happens is that, as you remain strong, even saying 'no' to their demands and continuing to put your needs in the position of prime importance, they then back down and accept that you are changing. They begin to appreciate this 'new you' while knowing that you are still who you are.

Level 3 - Enhancing Self-Care: This next level of self-care simply evolves from having regular, sustaining self-care activities in your life. You will find that as you get used to taking better care of yourself on a regular basis, it becomes more effortless. You will begin to look around and see life differently. You will begin to see yourself at the center in your own life, rather than on the edge looking in. Feeling and being more in charge – and letting go of the need of being in control – will occur. When you make plans for yourself, you are less likely to put them aside and deny yourself based on the needs and demands of others. 'Healthy Selfishness' becomes a healthy way of life, and you have a self-care attitude as a foundation for living. Noticing and experiencing joy will occur more frequently. People who used to control your life will have less impact on your mental wellness and energy levels. All of this evolves from having regular, sustaining self-care in your life!

When choosing self-care that really enhances your life begins, you will be moving in to the process of real transformation in your life. What will occur at this point is that you become motivated and energized through discovering who you are. You'll begin to choose activities, people and self-care strategies in your life based on their ability to help you stay positive and move forward in your life. The choices that you make will be ones that will propel you forward in your self-care, and in discovering and uncovering the real you. Your energy levels and ability to focus and get the job done will be easier, and stress will have less of an impact on you. And, you will find that you will be able to do this while living your normal life and getting the job done!

Level 4 - Transforming Self-Care: As you see, there is a real shift in how you see and take care of yourself as you move from Sustaining to Enhancing self-care practices. Self-care actually becomes easier at the Enhancing level as it has become a regular part of your life. You have retrained your body to know that you do not want to go back. If there are times of great stress and high demands, and you find that you are again using and depending on Survival strategies, you quickly bounce back to the level of Enhancing self-care. This happens simply by asking:

'How can I respond and not react to what is happening in my life?'

Transforming self-care is about choosing and following through on what you need to do to make some profound changes in your life and on how you care for yourself. The intention of transforming self-care is to enable change to occur, so that you are living a life most closely aligned to your true soul self, and what you really desire and deserve. You will find that self-defeating thinking becomes increasingly rare in your life, and that you are better able to 'make happen' or manifest what you need. Your ability to attain your goals quickens, and success as you define it readily occurs.

Shifting your attitude and perspective to yourself does not leave you alone, guilty, or feeling selfish. Rather, it is a process of transformation and an amazing way to have your needs and desires fulfilled. If you found that you can only identify with Survival self-care right now, and even doubt that your life could move to another level, it is important to gently accept that this is your starting point. Accept that with resolve and the commitment to yourself that a shift can happen in your life, and achieving your goals will become much easier.

Blocks to Building a Self-Care Attitude

What can really impact a woman's ability to take this journey and transform her life are self-defeating beliefs that are carried about self-care. There are six of them that are predominant. By knowing them and bringing them to your awareness, it will be easier to overcome them and not let them defeat you.

The Opinions of Others: One of the greatest blocks to incorporating a self-care attitude in to your life is the opinion of others. Now, these others could be a spouse, partner, parent, friend or child – anyone whose viewpoint matters to you. Sometimes, this creates an inner conflict, as these are the people that you assume would be the most supportive of your efforts, yet they put up the greatest roadblocks. And, if you are really having some challenges with incorporating self-care, then you may actively seek out others and listen to their viewpoints that support your resistance.

The strategy to get around this is to use a 'filter'. Whenever you communicate, there is a filter between the speaker and the listener, and it sifts out some of what is being said and heard. This usually reflects what you do not want to hear and, sometimes, only lets information through that fits with your own viewpoint. You can use this filter to your advantage when dealing with people who question your desires and goals. Use it with regard to challenges that you receive about the self-care choices you are beginning to make. Using this filter will also alert you to anyone who is trying to pull you away from your goals.

Beliefs about Survival Self-Care: We have learned to believe that self-care is simply about what we need to do to cope and survive. We have not yet learned to believe that self-care is the foundation for well-being, growth and success. It is about shifting your belief system and knowing that you need to develop a self-care attitude in your life.

The issue of 'feeling deserving' often comes up for women trying to make this shift. One of the ways we have learned to live our lives is to put our needs and desires behind those of everyone else. In turn, we believe that we can only address our needs and desires after others have been satisfied. We allow them to be in the power position with regard to our energy. This may seem simplistic in nature, so begin to assess it when it is in action. When you find that others are making requests of you, and even pulling on your energy to do what they want, see how this dynamic really does work in the day-to-day reality of your life.

The 'I Can Cope' Attitude: In the chapter on self-defeating thinking, you will learn how powerful our thoughts are, and that our body believes whatever our brain tells it. You will also learn Self-Coaching skills and find that there are times when there is real value in using phrases such as 'I can cope' when having too much to deal with at one time.

Yet as women, we overuse this phrase! We use it so frequently that is has become a block to real self-care. By saying and believing that "I can cope" we can deny our personal needs in the moment and stop ourselves from asking for assistance for others. When we use this phrase as a usual part of getting through the day, we become stuck in the belief of being a 'super-woman', and to be one, you must deny your need for self-care. Simply notice how often you use this phrase and how you feel when you do. You may find that you can plow ahead, but at the same time be very disconnected from yourself.

The 'I'll do it Later' Position: Once you embrace self-care, there is no going back. You will begin to feel and see the positive results in your life and reap the benefits. Recall that in the second level of self-care — Sustaining — the issue of slipping back and giving up your gains was addressed. One of the most common phrases or sayings that a woman hears when the pull to slip back begins is 'I'll do it later'.

Reflected in this is the belief that we have that our needs can be met after everyone else or after someone has given permission to do what 'I' need for myself. When you find that you begin putting off taking care of yourself and making excuses for not addressing what you need, that 'slipping back in to the survival mode' is imminent. Ensure that you do what you need to keep your needs paramount. Know that even if in reality, the demands on your life are high, you must ensure that you will get back to that sustaining level of self-care as soon as possible.

The Belief that 'I am Flawed if I need Self-Care': Throughout this book, we address how we have learned to accept that we have to keep up the illusion of having it all together, all of the time regardless of the reality of our lives. This creeps in to how we treat our bodies, do our work and keep our homes. This belief also creeps in to whether we have self-care in our lives on a regular basis or not, and how we treat ourselves in the process.

Know that there is nothing wrong with you if you need to improve your self-care. Know that there is nothing wrong with you if at times you feel like you need a great deal more than at other times. Know too, that there is nothing wrong with looking for help, support and nurturing outside of yourself with regard to your self-care. This could mean seeing a health or complementary wellness practitioner on a regular basis. Applaud yourself for your efforts, your follow-through and your kindness to yourself. Being able to accept your needs without self-judgment is central to being a successful woman.

The 'I Don't have the Time or Money' Belief: This is one of the greatest reasons why a woman believes that she cannot take better care of herself. You may feel like there are not enough hours in the day in your life. You also may believe that self-care is only available to you if you can spend a weekend in a spa or visit a resort. Believing that self-care can be part of our daily life (with minimal time needed and without any cost) may not fit with your current picture of what self-care means. Self-care techniques that do not take any time, can be done almost anywhere, and are free can be incorporated in your life – especially in times of high stress. Doing them reduces the risk of your stress building inside and leading you to 'blowing-up' at others as a result.

The following list of 10 Instant Self-Care Skills will help you get on the right track, and provide immediate strategies for you to use. As an exercise at the end of the chapter, there will be space for you to add your own original skills – they are as limitless and creative as you are!

Instant Self-Care Skills

1) **Breathing.** When we are feeling stressed, we hold our breath. We tend to breathe in the upper part of our chest, which gives our body the message that there is cause to feel anxious or scared. Simply notice how you are breathing. Gently say to yourself "remember to breathe", and slowly and deeply inhale.

2) **Enhanced Breathing:** To build upon #1, begin by gently breathing deeply into your body, and doing a few quick release breaths. Then place your hands on the following areas of your body and breathe deeply three times or more into that area: your upper chest, bottom of your rib cage, lower abdomen and bottom of the rib cage at your back. (Reach around to your back the best you can without strain.) This is a great exercise to practice at home, and becomes easier. It re-educates your body in effective breathing, and reduces back tension and strain.

3) **Ask yourself:** *'What is the best thing I can do for myself in this moment'?* Listen to your answer. If it is something you can do – all or in part – then do it! If it is not something you can do for yourself, play with the idea (see # 4).

4) **Optimal daydreaming.** Take a mental break by choosing to think about some relaxing or fun place that you would rather be.

5) **Taking off the blinders.** When we are stressed, we often walk with our eyes looking towards the floor. This accentuates tension and actually contributes to negative thinking. By looking up and looking around you, you stop this stress producing behavior. Follow-up by noticing three things that appeal to you. Then, notice how looking at them creates a sense of calm in your body.

6) **Thumping Your Thymus.** Your thymus is a gland in the centre of your upper chest. By "thumping" it you jump-start its function and increase your energy. Use the middle three fingers on your hand to sharply tap the centre of your chest in a counter clockwise circular motion. This means taping in the center of your chest up towards your left shoulder, and moving towards your right shoulder. Repeat this circular motion on the centre of your chest for a minute or more. You may notice your breath release as a sign of being finished.

7) **Permission to do Nothing:** Give yourself permission to sit and do absolutely nothing for at least one minute. Disconnect from your brain chatter (imagine it going in one ear and out the other), and sit still. Breathe deeply and gently (see #2). Doing nothing is not a passive act!

8) **Using Symbols:** Wherever you spend your time each day, make sure that there are symbols in view which hold meaning and beauty for you (i.e. a picture, photo, knick-knack, crystal, candle). When you look at it, it provides you an immediate sense of relaxation and a mini-break. (Making sure that your symbol or object contains inspiring colors such as orange, yellow, and red can also help.)

9) **Keep aromatherapy tools handy.** Essential oils are extracts made from plants that have been found to have healing qualities. Each extract has its own specific purpose depending on its plant source. Some of the most common ones for women are lavender (uplifting and relaxing), geranium (balancing and relaxing), and rosemary (balancing energy, and for hormonal issues). Speak with an aromatherapist about this, or visit your local health food store for alternatives and more information.

10) **Inspiring Words:** Keep a book of quotes with you that have meaning for you and keep you on track. These quotes can be motivational, spiritual or work-focused — as long as they have an uplifting meaning for you! Put them in a place handy to you throughout your day, and dip into them whenever you feel the desire.

Exercise: Energizing Your Self-Care Attitude

Part 1): Here are five beliefs that block a woman's ability to create a self-care attitude and foundation for her life. In the space below, write about the one(s) which are most present in your life and have an impact on you. How do they create a block that you would like to undo in your life?

➤➤ *Influence by the Opinions of Others*

➤➤ *The "I'll do it Later" Position*

➤➤ *The "I Can Cope" Attitude*

➤➤ *The Belief that "I am Flawed if I need Self-Care"*

➤➤ *"But I Don't have the Time or Money"*

_____

_____

_____

_____

_____

_____

Part 2): List instant stress-busting skills that you currently use, or ones that you would like to try. Refer to the list in this book and your own list when stressed and feeling the need to better care for yourself.

_____

_____

_____

_____

_____

_____

I know God will not give me anything I can't handle.
I just wish He didn't trust me so much.

- Mother Teresa of Calcutta

Chapter 5

Eliminating Self-Defeating Thoughts that Block Success

**Observing your thoughts and reducing
the self-defeating ones immediately reduces
stress and accelerates success.**

The most effective and quick way for a woman to be all she can be is through becoming an observer of her own thoughts. Most women engage in thinking that is self-defeating and are often not even aware of it! The reality is that your body believes whatever your brain tells it. Your brain is like a central processing unit of a computer, and will only work with the data that you give it. So, if your thoughts about yourself and what you are trying to attain are not as focused, clear and supportive as possible, then you are actually creating blocks to your own success.

Self-defeating thoughts are ways that we think which criticize our qualities, abilities, efforts, and desires. They have a specific intent. And this word 'intent' means that they have a particularly self-defeating purpose. Self-defeating thoughts can be a way of directly putting yourself down, being too critical, self-questioning or even denying what you have accomplished. They are a drain of our energy that can be seen as a disease in the lives of women today.

Do you ever feel like you are thinking constantly? Do you ever find that you are frustrated by the continual words and phrases going on in your head? The bottom-line is that this brain chatter often is overwhelming, and we wish there were a way to shut it off. This is something we all do as women, yet it is something that we never talk about. We have learned that it is a taboo subject. We feel incredibly embarrassed when we think that others may actually find out about the chatter and conflict in our thoughts, especially with regard to some of the things we say to ourselves about ourselves. Self-defeating thoughts:

▶▶ Fragment us from who we really are

▶▶ Keep us unaware of what we really need

▶▶ Camouflage how we really feel, and

▶▶ Stop us from hearing what our intuition is telling us.

Now these self-defeating or negative thoughts can be directed at others, at ourselves or at whatever we are trying to accomplish. For our purposes, we will focus on how our thinking impacts upon us directly as women.

> **When we reduce the ways that we create blocks to our own success, then – almost like magic – work and life challenges begin to flow more smoothly, and a sense of real well-being is present every day of our lives.**

The Outcome of Self-Defeating Thinking

We actually have some misunderstandings about our thought processes that block how effectively we think and how fully we use our creativity and intuition. These myths about our thoughts keep us believing that all of our thoughts, feelings and even our intuition must be rational and logical. We believe that if they do not make sense, our thoughts have no value. The analytical, rational way we have learned to think, and the high value that we have placed upon thinking this way all of the time can actually keep us more stressed and less focused in our lives.

Brain chatter and self-defeating thinking also stops us from using the powerful tool of our intention. Using our intent is like having a laser beam directed at what we wish to accomplish. It really adds focus to our purpose. When we can put our energies toward a goal with pure intent, we:

➤ Directly tap in to our inner resources

➤ Strategically choose how to attain our goals

➤ Utilize our energy to our advantage.

When self-defeating thinking occurs, we are then thrown off topic, our intent and the ability to be focused can be dramatically reduced. All in all, our power is minimized, and our strength is weakened. And our daily challenges are no longer hills, but feel like mountains! The most effective, efficient and direct way to reduce stress and increase focus is to understand self-defeating thinking and how it affects you.

> **Self-defeating thinking is any form**
> **of thought intended to put yourself**
> **or someone else down.**

Understanding self-defeating thinking with regard to busting stress is about becoming aware of how you think about stress and when you experience stressful situations. Recall that you body believes whatever your brain tells it. Therefore, the first goal is to reduce any thoughts or thought patterns that you may have that led to an increase in stress when you are experiencing overload, crisis or fatigue. Then, to create and maintain proactive, supportive patterns of thinking which minimize and even eliminate the impact of toxic stress on you.

Common Threads of Self-Defeating Thinking

Let's look at some examples of self-defeating thinking that occur for women, especially in the workplace. These may not all be specific for you, nor may you experience them all of the time. Most women can identify with them and the power that this thinking can have over their lives.

The first example is that of the *'I Should Monster'*. This is the voice in your head that lists off all of the other things you should be doing while you are working on something else. It is that list that goes on and on, telling you that you should be doing something else, you should be somewhere else, or you should be doing a better job. As your body believes whatever your brain tells it, you become anxious and jumpy, often not able to concentrate on what you are currently doing.

The second example is the self-defeating thought of the *'I Can't Do Its'*. This one usually comes in when a challenge seems too great, when there are too many problems at once or, if you are living with chronic, high levels of stress. As you are working away, it begins to creep in to your awareness, saying things like, 'I'll never get all of this done', or, 'I don't know how to do this', or even 'I can't deal with these problems or solve all of this'. This is a very common pattern, and one that can stop you in your tracks. The minute you think or say 'I can't' your body does two things:

▸▸ It begins to energetically shut down, and

▸▸ You become more childlike in your thoughts and behaviors.

Listen to your next "I can't" and notice how old you actually feel!

A third example is that of the *"I Nevers"*. Think of the previous example of I can't, 'I never' also shuts down your body and actually puts a brick wall in front of what you are trying to attain. These 'I never' statements are often followed by thoughts of never doing things right or well enough. And just as powerful, we often are self-defeating when we think 'I never' with regard to other people. Examples include "I never get the credit I deserve" or "I never get a break". Again, that old brick wall immediately goes up, and it is a tough one to get down.

These are three common examples of self-defeating thinking that have become a disease in women's lives. (Later in this chapter, we will more fully explore the common patterns). At this moment, check in with yourself:

▶▶ Are you feeling tense or more tired?

▶▶ Are you experiencing brain chatter about self-defeating thinking?

▶▶ Do you feel that there is something wrong for having thoughts such as these?

These reactions are common occurrences for women who are beginning to acknowledge and address their self-defeating thinking. Know that each and every woman who wants to let go of these powerful blocks to her success has this same experience.

The Taboo About Self-Defeating Thinking

These feelings often stem from the taboo that we have about talking about self-defeating thinking. This taboo has two sources. One is that: 'If I acknowledge it, then others will find out how I think about myself.' We use a lot of energy to keep this to ourselves. As you go through your day, notice the women around you and know that almost 100% of them engage in this type of thinking at one time or another — and many of them daily, if not constantly. The second taboo has its roots in our beliefs about our personal power. Part of our socialization as women has been to deny how intelligent, creative, and intuitive we really are. One of the ways that this repressed learning stays in place is through our use of self-defeating thinking. You see, beliefs about ourselves are strong forces inside of us and guide our actions, attitudes, energy and even the goals that we set for ourselves. Our self-defeating thinking keeps the belief that woman cannot be powerful in place. By reducing self-defeating thinking, you challenge this belief. Our core beliefs don't necessarily like to be challenged even when they are pulling us down. Know that, through reducing your brain chatter you will be learning to look at yourself and your inner gifts and talents in a new way – and this new way will propel you towards the goals that you wish to attain.

Know, too, that reducing self-defeating thinking is one of the most direct ways for a woman to increase her energy. The goal of this process is like the slogan for recycling: reduce, reuse, and recycle. Reduce the amount and impact of your negative thinking. Reuse your brainpower for more effective, productive thoughts. Learn to recycle what you 'hear' through the negative thinking, to begin to understand what it is really trying to tell you. You'll find that you feel more energized as you begin working with your thoughts and begin applying some new strategies and experiencing results. Recall that your body believes whatever your brain tells it, so as the negative decreases your energy and your self-esteem will increase. You will find that you also become less judgmental of these thoughts and of yourself. You will also discover your own original ways of working with them.

So, developing self-awareness when experiencing stress is the key to being able to feel in charge while the world whirls around you. The first step is to become an 'Observer of Your Own Thought Processes'. In this next section, you will learn more about how to do this, and reduce your self-defeating thinking. There are also two exercises at the end of this chapter to assist you with this process.

Becoming an Observer of Your Own Thought Process

The following are seven tips to remember when learning to become an Observer of your own thought process. Being able to master this skill will not only help you in reducing stress, it also allows you to be aware of other self-defeating patterns you may have, assisting you in better understanding your needs and desires, and even opens up your ability to hear your intuition.

Tip #1 **Commit to listening to your thoughts:** Recall that having intention is like shining a powerful laser beam at your goals. Committing to tuning in and listening to your thought processes with the purpose of reduce self-defeating thinking provides such a beam.

Tip #2 **Set aside time to listen:** Though you often feel that there are not enough hours in the day, setting aside time to listen to how you think may seem like a waste of time. Actually, spending a few minutes each day will allow you to take charge and open up your energy in a new way. By taking time to listen, you become aware of the self-defeating patterns that have become entrenched, you reduce stress and fear, and know when self-coaching skills can be of assistance. Remember: your body believes whatever your brain tells it!

Tip #3 **Pay attention to the words and tone you hear:** Writing down the words and tone that you hear increases your ability to understand them and know the specific patterns that you have. Notice, too, if you hear someone else's voice (often the voice of someone who had authority over you at one time or at the present time).

Tip #4 **Do not judge what you hear:** We are quick to judge ourselves negatively and analyze the meaning of all we do. This does not help reduce self-defeating thinking - it actually adds another layer to it! Remember your self-defeating thinking is what you have learned to do, and you are in the process of re-learning.

Tip #5 **Become an observer in the chaos:** The optimal time to listen to your thoughts is when your feel overwhelmed and in crisis. This is usually when self-defeating thoughts go in to overdrive

– stimulated by your anxiety or fear. Self-coaching (later in this chapter) and Instant Self-Care Skills (chapter 4) may be the real remedy that you need.

Tip #6 **Find the patterns:** We only have five or six patterns of self-defeating thinking. When under stress, the same patterns get repeated over and over. Be aware of what they are, so you will notice them when they begin. You will prevent them from spiralling out of control, which leads to greater stress.

Tip #7 **Reward yourself:** Learning your self-defeating patterns is a process, so do not expect to reduce them overnight. Reward your efforts!

Remember that this is probably new learning for you and, like all new learning, you need to put it into action. Work with the previous pointers, and you will be well on your way to being a very effective observer of your thoughts. As soon as you begin to observe your thoughts, you begin to take charge of how they impact your energy, focus and your life.

The following information will help you with this process. It outlines the top seven patterns of self-defeating thinking for women, and gives you examples of each. Remember, that you are in the process of letting go of the old, taking in the new, and integrating this into your life. Be gentle with yourself, and know that undoing these patterns will open up your energy, and allow you more effective use of your inner resources. Recall, too, that totally eliminating negative thoughts is not the goal nor possible in our busy lives. The goal is to reduce your self-defeating thinking so that the best of you can shine through.

The Eight Most Common Self-Defeating Thought Patterns for Women

Nighttime Racing
Perfection Thinking
Black and White Thinking
Name Calling
Body Conflict Thinking
Inadequacy Thinking
Out of Proportion Thinking
Fear of Change Thinking

Nighttime Racing

Many people most easily identify that their negative thinking occurs when they lie in bed, physically exhausted, ready for sleep. It is then that the Indy 500 of brain chatter starts to run in our heads. Repetitive, relentless words and phrases about how inadequate we feel about the day which is ending, the *'I should'* list which rambles on, and worry about tomorrow all seem to happen at the same time.

The number one thing to remember when dealing with this nighttime brain chatter is not to fight it. You may find your body trying to control it, with frustration and anger further stopping your attempts to sleep. The following suggestions may help. First, get out of bed, because you are not sleeping anyway. The traditional glass of milk or a protein-based snack may help. In addition, take out a piece of paper or your journal book if you keep one. Write down as quickly as you can all of the words and worries that are going through your mind. Keep writing until you feel the energy dissipate, and you begin to relax.

The key is to write it all down, and put it aside with a commitment to look at it the next day. Then, you must take a look at the list the next day, reading it over and reflecting on what you wrote on the list. You will probably find that what was a major issue the night before, really is not a problem in the light of day, or has found its own solution. You will be pleasantly surprised. Now, if you have chronic or long-term nighttime racing, doing this writing and reviewing exercise over a few days will be a big step in ending this problem. Doing the exercise over several days retrains your body to know that all that chatter keeping you awake is no longer an effective way to deal with the challenges and worries of the day. Try it, it works!

Perfection Thinking

The next pattern that can really plague women and really becomes a problem in times of stress is that of Perfection Thinking. Do you ever think 'I can never do it well enough' or 'Why do I even try, it's not right'? Do you ever look at something you have finished, or something that you are wearing, and rather than looking at the whole, see some small thing which is 'just not right'? Do you ever struggle with trying to 'figure out' the reason why you did something? These are examples of the perfection pattern of self-defeating thinking, and as women, this is a real specialty of ours!

It robs women of energy in several ways. One is that a job never seems quite done. Instead of owning an accomplishment, a woman caught in perfection thinking focuses on what needs to be done instead, or could be done better. This really throws time management out the window! Perfection thinking at work also makes it more difficult to present an idea or project to someone else, as you never quite think it is good enough. Another problem it creates is that it becomes much more difficult to delegate to others. When a person – especially a manager – is caught in perfection thinking, it becomes nearly impossible to think that someone else can complete the task as efficiently as you can.

Being an observer of your thoughts and developing self-awareness when you are engaged in perfection thinking is the key. Avoid judging, or being harsh on yourself when you begin to become aware of how you are thinking. Rather, reframe what and how you are thinking, so that you see the bigger picture. Focus on really owning what you are accomplishing in life. Remember to see the cup half full, rather than half empty.

Black and White Thinking

This pattern can really leave women stuck and cut off from their creativity and intuition. Black and White Thinking basically goes like this: 'If I don't see things one way, then it must be the other.' It is as though you only see two options to a situations or solutions to a problem. Usually, black and white thinking is about seeing things in extremes, and judging them as polar opposites. In terms of thinking about ourselves, it is usually about judging ourselves as one way or another. Examples include: 'If I am not thin, then I must be fat' or 'I must be lazy if I don't get everything done.'

Minimizing black and white thinking is about beginning to see the middle or neutral ground. When you begin to do this, you will find that you will use your energy in a more balanced way, as you will not be swinging between one extreme thought or another. Remember, your body believes whatever your brain tells it.

Name Calling

One of the most profoundly self-defeating (and one of the simplest to remedy) patterns of brain chatter is known as Name-calling. We will often call ourselves names that we would not allow other people in our life to call us. It often occurs when we are stressed, or if a situation is not going as well as we expected. Calling ourselves names zaps our energy. Common examples are: stupid, idiot, jerk, bitch, and dummy – and the list goes on – as creative as you are!

Body Conflict Thinking

The fifth pattern of self-defeating thinking that is especially harmful to our overall well-being is Body Conflict Thinking. Women's anxieties about their bodies run deep. Negative thinking about body shape, size, strength or weight has a very powerful hold over us. For some women, this type of brain chatter seems to be a constant throughout their day.

Sometimes, these thoughts about our bodies are fleeting and barely noticed. Yet, sometimes these thoughts have an abusive tone, which tears us to shreds. Until recently, body conflict thinking was most often an issue for women. Now, men too have begun to believe that their body size or body type is somehow inadequate. Recall that your body believes whatever your brain tells it. If you are overly critical of yourself through body conflict thinking, then your energy, focus and enjoyment of each day can really be affected and distorted.

Inadequacy Thinking

The next pattern is that of Inadequacy Thinking. In the briefest possible moment, you can have a thought that states clearly what you need, how you feel, where you would like to go, or what you would like to have. In such moments, you experience incredible clarity and insight, and feel powerful and on top of the world. In such a moment, everything feels as if it has come together, and you are truly living in that moment. Then, another thought comes in which puts you down, questions your judgment, or denies your decision-making. In a flash, you move from this sense of being powerful and successful to that of being down and really feeling inadequate. You can easily lose direction, and can even take away from yourself what you are trying to achieve.

Out of Proportion Thinking

The seventh pattern of self-defeating thinking is called Out of Proportion Thinking. This type of self-defeating thinking is about thinking in a way that distorts reality. This pattern is not so much about what you say in your head, but rather the process of how thinking about yourself gets out of control. A clear example of out of proportion thinking is with regard to thinking about what someone said to you that you felt hurt over. As you think of the situation over and over again, it grows and grows until you feel really angry, frustrated or hurt. It has been blown out of proportion through focusing on it too much. 'Out of proportion thinking' may also be part of your other patterns, especially self-directed name-calling and body conflict thinking. Be aware of how you can create additional stress for yourself by allowing your thoughts to run away with you.

Fear of Change Thinking

This eighth form of self-defeating thinking has a different flavor than the other seven types, and occurs at a different time. Yet, it is just as powerful, and will stop us in our tracks from moving forward in life.

By using the information and techniques in this book and practicing other types of wellness approaches, your life will begin to change and evolve in a fast-forward mode. You will be more focused, attain your goals more easily and have greater inner peace and less stress. What often occurs when these positive, uplifting changes begin to occur is that our body goes in to fear mode. That's right – when you finally start to get what you really want, fear can kick in and undermine the process. This fear can lead you to feel immobilized. In turn, you can fall into old patterns or ways of behaving that are not supportive of the new you, and how you desire to do things now.

You see, there is a part of us that fears change. We've been taught to experience this in life, and it can be connected with the need to control, and our sense of being deserving. So, it is important to know that this can occur when things seem to be going their best. Recognize it for what it is, and do not get caught up in the power of your self-defeating thoughts and use them against yourself. Keep positive and focused on your goal while really supporting yourself and your efforts.

Exercise #1: Accelerating Your Observational Abilities

Becoming an Observer of Your Own Thoughts also involves connecting to the emotional impact of an issue at hand. Not recognizing how we feel about something can block our energy and keep us stuck in repetitive, self-defeating thinking. This is a great exercise to use whenever you find that you are stuck on an issue, or overly focused on a particular person.

Down the left side, write down the word that best represents the issue. In this case, money is used, as most people have some issues regarding money. Within a time frame – could be 5, 10 or 15 minutes – write down every word you can think of that starts with a particular letter in the word. So for 'M' you could write: more, marvelous, misplace, etc. Do this for all of the letters as quickly as you can and do not censor your answers. Write the first thing that pops into your head. Then review your answers and look at the themes. Are their indicators of how your thoughts and feelings are keeping you stuck on the issue?

M_____

O_____

N_____

E _____

Y_____

Exercise #2: Reducing Self-Defeating Thinking Exercise

Becoming an observer of your own thoughts is the critical first step to reducing self-defeating thinking. Stop fighting with it. Remember trying to tell it to stop when trying to sleep?) Instead, begin to recognize it and the patterns in a non-judgmental, observer-type way. The following exercise will help you begin to recognize your patterns, and work with them to reduce their presence.

1) List the phrases or put-downs you often hear yourself saying, or find yourself thinking, especially when stressed.

_____

_____

_____

_____

_____

_____

2) With each one, what tone of voice or whose voice do you hear?

_____

_____

_____

_____

_____

_____

3) **In the space below, summarize the results from #1 and #2.** Do you see any patterns in the words or phrases that you use? Do you see any patterns in the tone that you use or hear, e.g. harsh, critical, childlike, whiny?

_____

_____

_____

_____

_____

_____

The Hidden Meaning:

Critical or harsh phrases mean that you need a break. You are putting too much pressure on yourself, being overly responsible, or working too hard. Stop whatever you are doing, take a break and come back to the problem or situation. Imagine a bird flying in the air and how they see things – look at the bigger picture.

Inadequate thoughts are an indicator that you need some nurturing. As you are feeling this way, it will be very hard to get anything done. Take a break in the moment, plan something that is nurturing for you, and refer to the section in this book on self-care for further assistance.

Chapter 6

Self-Coaching and the Power of Limitless Thinking

Being your own best friend augments your successes, and lights the way for your limitless potential to unfold.

The next step in our *Successful Woman* program focuses on developing self-coaching skills. They involve inserting positive, affirming statements into your thought patterns. Several positive things occur as a result:

▶▶ There is less room and space for self-defeating thoughts.

▶▶ Your mind begins to think in a more focused, effective way.

▶▶ A powerful, affirming self-care attitude takes hold in your life.

As women, we are really good at taking care of everyone and everything else first – especially in acknowledging the accomplishments of others, and being supportive of their actions. We are not really good at doing this for ourselves. Becoming your own self-coach turns the tables so that you are being proactive about your needs and taking care of yourself. Your inner foundation is strengthened, and you send yourself the message that you are open to abundance and success in your life.

Everyone has seen or experienced a coach in action. We each have preconceived notions of who a coach is and how a coach should act. Yet, we do not always understand what makes a coach effective. A great coach is not someone who yells at the players and puts them down. An effective coach is a person who teaches, supports and motivates. An effective coach brings out the best in whomever they are working with. An effective coach is firm and focused, serving as a guide and a catalyst for change. She is energetic, and knows how to persevere with spirit in a non-judgmental way.

How often are we coaches for others, and how infrequently for ourselves?

Imagine walking around all day, every day, with an internal coach helping you remain focused, calm, and not reacting to stress. The keys to becoming your own self-coach are:

▸▸ Using positive, self-supportive statements or affirmations

▸▸ Transforming your self-defeating thinking

▸▸ Learning how to combine the two, and become a Coach Plus!

Keys to Becoming Your Own Self-Coach

Part 1: Using Self-Supportive Statements

In the self-help field over the past couple of decades, self-supporting statements or affirmations have become quite popular. They really do work. Their intention is to help you, in the moment, to counteract the negativity and stress that you are experiencing. Their intention is to create a solid foundation within yourself through noticing, owning, honoring and affirming who you are and what you need. When using affirmations, you learn to live from within yourself, and learn to assess what is helpful and supportive for you through the day. This not only reduces stress, but also builds greater self-esteem.

Who knows better than you what you really need to hear, to cope in the moment, and to move forward feeling energized?

A great way to begin doing this is for you to start focusing on your qualities. Our qualities are what make us unique, special and distinct as a person. In the hustle and bustle of life, women often forget their qualities. They forget that they have a certain something that is really special that they bring to each and every situation or encounter that they have. We are often in a 'doer mode' trying to get the job done, and do it in a way that disconnects from ourselves. To be successful in whatever your endeavors are, you need to be aware of your qualities.

Qualities are aspects such as humour, kindness, loyalty, generosity, focus, or creativity. These examples are simply a few. As you have found by completing the exercise in chapter 1, the list of qualities for each and every one of us goes on and on. To really affirm your qualities, when you notice one, say to yourself that you see it, recognize it, own it and value it. Own your uniqueness and wear it proudly!

Affirm your qualities by saying them to yourself over and over. Write them down so you remember what they are. Use them when you find that your brain chatter and self-defeating thinking is taking over, and taking you off focus. It may seem strange at first but, through affirming yourself, you increase your self-esteem and begin to see yourself in a new way.

How you think creates the reality of your life.

So, even if you have a hard time believing these affirmations at first, persevere and keep using them, and three things will happen:

▶▶ They become easier and you feel more energized.

▶▶ You begin to really own your uniqueness and, only then, are able to use your strengths to your advantage.

▶▶ Other people begin to notice how unique and effective you are. It is like a light goes on, and others begin to notice, appreciate and respect you, and this lays a foundation for greater success and ease in living.

The following exercise will help you develop self-supportive statements through owning and affirming your qualities.

Exercise: Strategies for Developing Self-Supportive Statements

Refer to your *Qualities Checklist* found in the first chapter. Below, on the left side, write your top three qualities. On the right side, create 'I' based statements which focus and affirm this quality. Keep in mind while creating them, that your intention is to use them as a self-coaching remedy while under stress. Example: Quality is curiosity. Statement: 'I am a curious person who uses this invaluable tool each and every day.'

Quality	Self-Supportive 'I' Statement
1.	1.
2.	2.
3.	3.

Part 2: Transforming Your Thought Patterns

Developing self-supportive statements or affirmations is the first remedy for reducing self-defeating thinking. So far, we have covered how to do this by noticing and affirming personal qualities. The second step in the process of reducing self-defeating thinking is through the transformation of thought patterns. Recall the seven top patterns of self-defeating thinking for women? Once you are aware of them, and recognize them, you can then begin to transform the impact that they have on your life.

The intent of affirmations and self-supportive statements is to help you provide a more solid inner foundation, and to really use your qualities to your advantage. In this second step, the transformation of thought patterns involves building upon your internal foundation with the intent of transforming your thought patterns, particularly when under stress. When you are able to do this, it stops self-defeating thinking from spiraling out of control, and stops stress from being reinforced and magnified. It is when these patterns are altered, that they become positive and self-supportive, and no longer detrimental or negative. You then grow and expand to attain a personal goal or move closer to your true potential. Recall that, sometimes, our self-defeating thoughts are providing clues and information as to the type of support or help that is needed. By transforming self-defeating thinking, you are using this information to your benefit, and meeting your needs and de-stressing.

The following is the story of Linda, and how her self-defeating thinking brought her defeat:

> *One morning, Linda was preparing for a job interview that she really desired and she had worked a long time to be considered for. As she was getting ready, she was nervous and worried and notices a pimple on her face. Her first thought was that "This pimple on my face is so gross. I bet that is all they will look at in my job interview today." On closer inspection, she*

said to herself, "My skin never looks nice, and I have a double chin," and then, "oh, does my face ever look fat." Her thoughts really became self-defeating when she thought: "Well, if I could lose weight, then I wouldn't look so fat" and then "Yech! My clothes are so tight; I look like a cow." Finally in her frustration, Linda said to herself: "I'll never get that job because I am too fat."

Can you identify with how Linda moved through a spiral of self-defeating thinking from having a pimple, to convincing herself that she will not get the job because her body is inadequate? Instead of sabotaging herself, Linda could have covered up the blemish, acknowledged her fears about the interview, boosted herself and her self-esteem with self-supporting statements, and headed off to her interview confident and self-assured. Instead, she talked herself out of the job she really desired.

Exercise: Transforming Your Thought Patterns

The intent of transformative statements is to alter your thought patterns when under stress, so that stress is not reinforced and magnified. Alter so that they become positive and self-supportive and no longer detrimental or negative. You then grow and expand to attain a personal goal or move closer to your true potential.

Below, in the left column, write out the self-defeating statements that you find happening when under stress. (Refer to your responses to the first question in exercise #2 under self-defeating thinking). There is room for up to five. In the right column, you are going to write a transformed statement. Asking yourself the following questions will help:

▸▸ *How can I turn around what I have been saying to make it a positive statement?*

▶▶ *How can I change my tone so that I sound less critical or helpless and more affirming?*

▶▶ *How can I best accept my qualities and abilities today?*

▶▶ *What is the most helpful thing that I can say to myself when under stress?*

▶▶ *What is the most supportive thing I can say to myself when under stress?*

▶▶ *What would a coach say to me when I am feeling frazzled and overwhelmed?*

What I Have Been Saying to Myself	What I Choose to Say Now
1.	1.
2.	2.
3.	3.
4.	4.
5.	5.

Your beliefs become your thoughts
Your thoughts become your words
Your words become your actions
Your actions become your habits
Your habits become your values
Your values become your destiny
~ Mahatma Gandhi

The Power of Limitless Thinking

We've learned that our thoughts create the life we live. They directly impact how we attain our goals, and how we see all the success we have in our lives now. Now, we are beginning to work on expanding your innate brainpower through teaching you how to more effectively focus your thoughts to increase your limitless thinking. Being able to think in this way is necessary for a woman to be able to do, to ensure success in her life and live in a more balanced way. Recall from the last section, that your body believes whatever your brain tells it. So, if you are thinking judgmental and limiting thoughts, your body will act them out. If you are thinking in an expanded way about your amazing skills and your unlimited potential, your body will act this out too — even attracting the success you desire.

With thinking in a more limitless way, you leave behind old behaviors and learning. You see your potential in a new way. Limitless thinking is also about:

▶▶ Expanding your thought capacity and problem solving ability.

▶▶ Increasing your inner vision about yourself and your life.

▶▶ Using the power of 'intention' more fully.

▶▶ Developing a pro-active attitude and letting go of judgment.

▶▶ Learning to think more creatively.

▶▶ Knowing your dreams and attaining your goals effortlessly.

Limitless thinking is a new way that brings together a woman's internal resources such as intelligence, creativity, and intuition with a goal-oriented approach. It is about owning your dreams, setting a course for attaining them, and using all of your resources to get there in a way that works for you in your life. It is about the pictures that you see, about your potential to actually become real. Limitless thinking is about enjoying the journey, and learning how to nurture yourself along the way. It is also about flexibility – how to alter the view of your goal to fit with your learning, yet not letting go of it.

Blocks to Limitless Thinking

The belief that we have about attaining goals and success is that we need to be 'driven' in both our thoughts and our behavior. Driven means that a goal is determined, and we do everything in our power to get there as directly as possible. Recall the story earlier in this book about the horse wearing blinders to effectively pull a buggy. This horse is only allowed to see what is ahead to quickly get to the destination. Delicious grass, vehicles, or other horses cannot distract it. Well, we're not horses! The number of roles we have, and the belief that we have to do it all reinforces our 'driven' beliefs. It is common for women to believe: 'I must be driven, or I won't get it all done'. Our 'driven' belief is also an unfortunate outcome of learning that the only form of effective thinking is one that is logical and rational. We learned to deny our feelings, which cut off limitless thinking potential. Add to this the fact that neither women nor men have received much encouragement for thinking and being creative, so that thought potential has been constrained.

> **Learning to think about yourself in a more limitless way is a radical act. Radical in that it will change the current reality of your life.**

Intention and Attitude

Using the power of intention and developing a non-judgmental attitude about yourself and others creates the foundation for limitless thinking. Intention is a focused purpose. It is about:

▸ Our ability to focus our desires, passion, and emotions on what we wish to attain.

- ▶▶ Focusing our energy on our goal in an unwavering way.

- ▶▶ Owning our desires and truly believing that they are valid – regardless of the opinions of others, and

- ▶▶ Connecting with our passion as the fuel for our intentional behavior.

If we have dreams and desires but no passion, it is like traveling in a canoe without the paddle. You may eventually get to your goal, but only if the current and the wind takes you that way. Emotions and passion are connected, and knowing your feelings about your goals are essential. Connect with which feelings will help you attain the goal – feel them in your body, and visualize what you wish to attain at the same time. Also work with the feelings that may be blocking your actions, such as fear, self-doubt, guilt, or anger. To help with this process of strengthening your intention, refer to the section on *10 Keys for Limitless Thinking* and the exercise at the end of this chapter.

Developing a proactive attitude goes along with using your intention to attain your goals. We've worked a great deal with becoming an observer of your own thoughts, and developing self-awareness about how you think and what you think about. A proactive attitude is similar in that you alleviate judgment about yourself, and you let go of judgment of others. We may believe that we are not judgmental and accepting, when we really tune into our thoughts we often find that this is not true. We have learned to have judgment about others as a way of feeling like we are protecting ourselves. We believe that by doing this, we can create a shield between ourselves and others and their actions. When doing this, what it really does is rob us of energy and focus. Keeping clear in our thoughts, and not judging others for their beliefs is the key.

Expand your Thoughts to Expand your Potential

Let's begin the journey of expanding your potential. Whether you have a particular goal in mind or not right now, learning these skills will change how you view yourself, and open up your potential for both being all you can be and having inner peace.

The first step is to own your dreams for yourself. Reread that sentence: it is a very powerful one. Women often know the dreams of their friends, life and work partners, and especially those of their children. You may have forgotten your own dreams, locked them away deep inside of you, or stopped yourself from having them. These dreams are not those of the nighttime. These are the hopes and aspirations that you had for yourself in your life: the pictures you had at one time about how you thought your life would be, and the woman you would become. Again, let go of any guilt you may feel about what you have done with your dreams – owning them again is new learning for all women.

To reconnect you with your dreams, let's briefly go back in time. Ask yourself the following questions (there is space at the end of this chapter for your responses):

▶▶ What were my dreams for my life as a young adult?

▶▶ Where are they now?

▶▶ How long has it been since I have thought about my dreams?

▶▶ How am I feeling about this?

You may be surprised with the awareness you have now, and how you may be feeling. All in all, women have learned three things about having dreams for their own lives:

1) **'I have to give them away'**: You have learned to give your dreams away and to believe that you can find fulfillment through taking on and supporting the dreams of others in your life. In this process, the whole notion of having dreams and following them is lost.

2) **'I have to keep my old dreams'**: We have learned that the dreams that we have as a child are the ones that we must keep. You may have already found that the dreams you had in your youth no longer fit for you as an adult woman. You may have also found that the ones you thought would work for you, really don't. In addition, the ones you learned to believe about being a woman and the life you were 'supposed to' have were not realistic, but were based on an outdated belief system about women's roles.

3) **'I cannot have new dreams for my life'**: You have grown and changed as a woman and are now on your journey of self-discovery. Your dreams have changed, yet you have not given yourself the permission to have new ones. You can develop and nurture new ones. You CAN and WILL develop new dreams now in your life and you have every right to follow them. Understanding and accepting this is the first step on the road to more limitless thinking in your life.

Dreams in the Daytime

Dreams in the daytime are very powerful tools for living. We have learned to call them 'daydreams', and we have learned to minimize their importance. We have learned to believe that they are a 'waste of time', and the notion of wasting time in our society is equal to breaking the law. You may also find some resistance to dreaming for yourself since, as women we have learned to equate their dreams in the day with worry. When an image or thought comes to mind that takes you out of your current situation, it is about a problem, a conflict, or a negative brain chatter. Our ability to dream during the day has been taken over by this force of negativity, and now it is time to reclaim its power and nurturing impact.

Dreaming during the daytime can happen anywhere, at any time. As you begin to have fun with them and experience their power, you will welcome them in more often in the day, and use them for self-care. Sometimes, they are as simple as getting lost in thoughts that take you away from a current situation to a place which feels better for you. These daydreams are usually seen as a picture in your mind's eye. They can also be experienced through any of your senses as a sound, touch, smell, taste or a feeling. Now, you will learn to use them in a guided way, with a purpose in mind.

Exercise: Recharging through Your Daydreams

You may want to start by setting aside a time and a place for your dreams during the day. It is not necessary, but it will help you to regain this creative part of yourself more quickly. Working with the following steps will give you a framework for this process. Keep in mind that there is no right or wrong about this, and will be based upon your individual needs, desires and pacing.

Step 1)   Pick a spot as the place where you go to daydream. You are looking for a place where you can be alone and there is some quiet. If you are not sure where that is, close your eyes and ask yourself: 'Where is the place I can go in my daily life to reclaim my dreams?' It may or may not be a place in your home, but it will be a place you are near on a regular basis. Remember, this exercise is limitless in itself, yet it may take a little practice.

Step 2)   Let your mind wander to the image of a place that is very nurturing for you. It can be somewhere you have visited as an adult or a child, or somewhere that you would like to go. It can also be a place that you create solely for yourself. In this space, there is only nurturing – anything that does not feed your soul is not allowed here.

Step 3) Use all of your senses to really be nurtured. Take in the sounds, smells, tastes, sights, and anything that you feel there. Let the peace and nurturing wash over you, and know that you can take this experience back with you to your day.

Step 4) Record your experiences and learning:

_____

_____

_____

_____

_____

_____

Persevering with this exercise can give you incredible results. In as little as five minutes, doing this can provide you with self-care during the day, and will even make solutions to problems come easier. The exercise following *'The Meaning of Money'* in chapter 9 builds on these skills to help you create more prosperity in your life.

10 Keys to Limitless Thinking for Women

1) **Know your self-defeating thought patterns:** In the previous chapter, you learned about the common thought patterns that women have that reduce energy, confidence, and potential. Be aware which of the patterns are specific to you. Notice how they will try to creep in whenever you begin to think about yourself in a new, larger way. Remember this is new learning, and the old learned patterns are no longer needed.

2) **Give yourself permission each day to think limitlessly:** You are reprogramming your brain and your body. When you wake up in the morning - even before getting out of bed – affirm yourself by saying at least 3 times:

   'I will think limitlessly about myself, my life and my potential today.'

   Repeat this statement throughout the day. It is easy to remember when you tack it on to another behavior repeated during the day, such as drinking water, having a coffee, or even going to the bathroom!

3) **Accept that you will feel when you think:** Thinking and feeling are separate yet intertwined. Your feelings are your feelings. Yet, how you think can create how you feel. (The next time you are angry, notice the thought you had before the feeling.) Recognize and own your feelings when you have them as blocking them will stop limitless thinking. You may even shed some tears, which, in turn, will undo an emotional block and lead to more limitless thinking.

4) **Say no. Make time to be alone:** These are often two of the most difficult and anxiety producing things for a woman to do. Know that once you begin to take time for yourself, and set limits on others, it becomes much easier. Also realize that doing this is a necessity, and not a luxury in your life. Quiet time and being alone are a necessary component to feeling relaxed and in charge of your life, and provides the door open to your limitlessness.

5) **Suspend self-judgment:** You are in the process of relearning how you think. Avoid judging yourself for the new thoughts that you have, and stop taking in the judgments of others. Do not let others silence you or stop the positive energy you are experiencing from flowing. As you begin to think differently about yourself, you will begin to act differently as well. You will stop asking for what you need and begin to do what you need. Know that others will judge you, and make comments about the 'new you'. Stick with what you know is right for you, and the vision or direction you have for yourself in your life.

6) **Ask for the input of others but listen to your own inner voice:** The input of others is important, especially if you need assistance in problem-solving and attaining your goals. Input does not mean listening to what someone else tells you, and then doing it. Input means you ask for the opinion and help of someone who is supportive and not judging you. It is about adding to your problem-solving resources in a way that works for you.

7) **Bring more creativity into your life:** Recall that we live in a time where we often believe that if something is not rational or logical, then it has no value. Doing something creative may not seem part of your 'to do' list, but by beginning to see yourself as creative, and owning the value of being creative, in your life, you will be more energized and limitless in your approach to life's challenges. (See Chapter 8.)

8) **Nurture your body:** You have begun doing this already by working to reduce how you use your negative thoughts against yourself. Incorporating self-care in your life expands your ability to think limitlessly. You are giving yourself the message that you are valuable and important.

9) **Carry a notepad or journal:** Women often get a 'flash' in their thoughts about a solution to an issue, or a direction for their lives while going through the motions of daily life. By always carrying a journal dedicated to capturing these thoughts, you will be gaining a wealth of information. It is important to write them in the moment whenever possible, for these rich thoughts are easily lost if you 'wait until later'.

10) **Know that you can put a time limit on your thinking:** Again, limitless thinking is not about thinking non-stop about an issue. This leads to confusion and frustration, and cuts off your inner wisdom and creativity. You can put a time-limit on how long you will think about an issue, or even when you are going to think about it. This is about setting internal limits on your thought processes, which actually gives you more energy and a feeling of freedom.

If you do not express your own original ideas,
If you do not listen to your own being,
You will have betrayed yourself.

- Rollo May

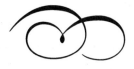

Chapter 7

Owning Our Emotional Strengths

**Owning our feelings is a proactive work
and life strategy for women.**

A woman's feelings are the doorway to her soul. A woman's feelings cannot be separated from the essence of whom she is. A woman's feelings are the truest indicator of her needs at any point in time. Yet, we have not learned to value our feelings. We have most often learned that they must be feared, shut down and not trusted. What a huge chasm this creates; a huge separation between our real nature and how we are supposed to live.

Feelings are the emotional experience of a sensation. As human beings, our ability to feel is a gift with which we are born. To feel is as natural, and as necessary as breathing or drinking water. We have great capacity to feel, and to use our feelings as beacons to guide us throughout life.

> Yet, we live in a time when we are only just beginning to emerge from an emotional Dark Ages. We are now awakening to the power of feeling, and its potential for teaching us to live in a limitless way.

As we grow, we are taught many things, yet are not taught about what feelings are, how to experience them nor how to let their knowledge guide us. Our race would not have survived without feelings. People learned rather quickly to use their anger to defend themselves from a threat, and to listen to their fear, and run when needed. Though we believe we have 'evolved', we are just beginning to understand and learn that our feelings are a cornerstone to who we are, and that they carry information crucial to our ability to survive and thrive.

So, here you are on a journey inward to learn to awaken and embrace this wonderful part of womanhood that has been denied. We have learned to label these 'sensations' as good and bad, positive and negative and right and wrong. We have learned to reject those that we consider wrong and uncomfortable and feel inadequate if we do not have positive ones at all times. What this has done is limited our full understanding of ourselves.

Accept that you have probably learned many lessons about having and expressing how you feel, but very few role models showing you how to own this part of who you are. You may even feel some anxiety, excitement, or both while reading this, for this feeling part of yourself is long dormant and wants to reawaken. This process of transformation cannot be experienced in the mind – it needs to be experienced in the body as this is where our feelings live. So, while you are reading this chapter and working with the exercises, you will have some body-based experiences. Connect with what you feel while you read, as doing this is part of the process of healing and feeding a woman's soul.

Celebrating Your Emotions

Now is the time to begin celebrating our emotions: to experience joy about how we feel, and when we feel, rather than shutting off our feelings. Time to affirm ourselves by saying:

"My feelings are real and valid.
Knowing this opens the door to
uncovering my true essence."

Own your feelings, hear them, revel in them, and let them be your guide. Greater inner peace and greater abundance will be the result. (While writing this, I felt compelled to shout this from a mountaintop.) The time is here-and-now to accept the power and wisdom gained through owning our *emotional self*.

We are living in a time when we are beginning to give ourselves permission to feel. This means we believe that we are supposed to:

▶▶ Know how to let ourselves feel,

▶▶ Have the ability to hear and understand what our feelings are trying to tell us,

▶▶ Be comfortable in expressing our feelings in an effective and safe way, and

▶▶ Know how to use our feelings in a proactive way.

> **Feelings are the emotional experience of body-based sensations that provide us with information. 'Body-based' means that we experience feelings physically, and, they can be stored throughout our bodies.**

This is important to know because we often only associate feelings with the heart, yet they are experienced throughout the body. Our feelings actually provide us with 'non-empirical' information. This means that feelings cannot be proven – there is no external, material evidence of their existence. We can see someone's expression of a feeling, but it does not prove that it exists. Yet, feelings are very real.

Experiencing and expressing feelings are truly an individual experience.

Even more importantly, feelings are the voice of the soul. They speak to us, letting us know how we are experiencing life, what we need in order to be fully nurtured. They provide a guide to what we need in our lives emotionally. In turn, when we listen, our soul is fed. Thus, when a feeling arises, it is providing information about our outer life and needs, but also it is providing information about what our real *inner self* needs to thrive. It provides us with this information so that we can be truly limitless in our lives, and on our personal growth journey.

Experiencing emotions – and our understanding of them in our lives – is a huge part of owning and using our inner resources and strengths in creating lives that have real meaning for us, the sense of balance that we need, and the success that we deserve. We experience life more fully alive. We believe that we can only experience what is comfortable for us, or what is experienced as uplifting – joy, excitement, peacefulness, motivation. And in turn, we believe that we should avoid at all costs those feelings that we do not experience as comfortably by us, such as fear, anger, sadness, or remorse. There is the real value today that anything unpleasant needs to be judged as not good and rejected. Yet, this does not work well for our emotional health.

Recall that energy is about pep or physical stamina, and is about the flow of life force through our bodies. When we deny that we have emotional responses, an energy blocks are actually created in the body. As a result, the flow of energy is stifled. Understand that this does not mean that you express whatever you are feeling any way that you like.

Accepting how you feel, and then choosing how you express it,
are two different things.

This is about knowing that when you try to ignore or deny how you feel, you are actually robbing yourself of energy and wellness.

Along with this, intuition often makes an appearance through our experience of our emotions. How you feel can be the speaker for your inner knowing, and the information that your own inner wisdom is trying to share. In an upcoming chapter in this book, you will learn about intuition. This inner knowing can come to us loud and clear through a feeling that will not go away or one that strongly makes its presence known.

Beliefs about Feeling

So, how did we learn to shut ourselves down emotionally? Well, doing this once had a purpose. Our ancestors, for the most part, lived in survival mode. All of their energies and focus needed to be on providing for the basic necessities of life each and every day. Feelings needed to be suppressed in order to continue to move forward and work. We have been experiencing a shift in consciousness about our lives and ourselves. This shift has moved many of us away from using our energy for basic survival, so we have the energy and ability to look more deeply into our human experience and ourselves. Now, we can give ourselves permission to feel.

Impeding this process of opening up emotionally are our long held beliefs about feeling. Our beliefs are very powerful and are, for the most part, forces out of our awareness that dictate how we live our lives. We have heard lots of these messages about feeling and expressing how we feel, and, particularly for us as women, we have internalized them and made them part of our belief system, about experiencing them. These common beliefs about feeling are:

Common Belief #1: 'I invent my feelings': We do not create how we feel in any given moment. Often this belief comes to us through our brain chatter when we hear 'You are making that up'. The reason we do this is that if we are creating how we feel, then we do not have to take our feelings or ourselves seriously. In turn, we can allow others to reinforce these false beliefs in our lives. Have you ever had the experience of being told you are 'making it up' when trying to express how you feel? This can silence a woman very quickly. Silence is the outcome as confidence is shattered and shame can arise.

Feelings can move us quickly to action when something is not right for us. As long as we deny how we feel, we deny ourselves, and are unable to embrace and use our personal power. We do not invent how we feel. What can happen is that our thoughts can distort how we are feeling. This can happen as a result of:

▶▶ Our thoughts about the other person or situation.

▶▶ A release of old, hidden emotions piggy-back on the current issue in search of release.

▶▶ A physical imbalance, illness or hormonal shifts.

Here's an example of how this works: *If I find that I am anxious about a new challenge, and I dwell endlessly on it and on how I feel, anxiety can grow through fear to terror about the situation. The anxiety is still there, but distorted thinking has created the terror.*

Common Belief #2: 'I should keep my feelings to myself': This is a factor in the inner struggle about our emotions that we feel now. We are living in a time when we have permission to talk about our feelings, yet we get stuck if we try to do it.

Life experiences and relationship issues often give a person the message that it is 'safer' to stay quiet. A person may experience trying to express their feelings and assume it backfires. This assumption usually happens when a person reacts rather than responds to what is being said. The automatic conclusion is: "It is better not to express myself." Self blame is easy in this situation when it really takes two to communicate effectively – a speaker and a non-judgmental listener.

Taking this one step further, women and men who experienced abuse or assault may have learned directly that expressing their feelings led to physical hurt and pain – and pain is a real teacher. So, their deep learning was *'It is safer to stay quiet.'* In this way, they miss the chance to learn that there are 'safe' people to whom they can express their feelings.

Common Belief #3: 'I need to control how I feel': This belief is based on the value that we need to be 'in control' of our feelings at all times. Control really means having power over someone or something. When we live life trying to control others, it means we have to have power over them somehow.

The same goes for feelings. But whenever we try to control feeling, an internal power struggle is created. The outcome is often that a person feels disconnected and out of control!

The goal is to be 'in charge' of how we feel and how feelings are expressed. In charge 'I' have found ways in my life for the effective expression of them. *It means that I do not let my feelings rule my life and my actions, but rather I use the information they provide to guide my life and decisions.*

Common Belief #4: 'I need to 'let go' of my feelings': The phrase 'let it go' is heard a great deal today. Doing this has some value, yet it also has some danger to it – particularly for women. If you immediately say *'I'll just let go of this'* when feeling something uncomfortable, then you may be shutting down the experience of feeling.

> **When you deny your feelings, you deny yourself. Feelings are energy. If a strong feeling arises, and you deny it, it will return.**

The feeling regarding a particular experience will come back until it is experienced, listened to, and somehow worked through. This is the downside of believing that you can let go of an uncomfortable or painful feeling. However, there is a point in the process of working through difficult feelings when it is time to surrender and let go of their impact upon you. You release their presence in your life. This needs to come at a time when the energy of the feelings has dissipated – usually through experiencing them, and doing some conscious work to move through them. When you hold on to feelings past their 'shelf life', resentment has a chance to form and take hold. Resentment is one of the most damaging emotions for your esteem, your relationships and our health. Resentment only hurts you.

Common Belief # 5: 'I have learned that feelings have no value': This belief centres on the fact that we cannot see feelings nor 'prove' that they are real. Believing feelings have no value conflicts with giving ourselves permission to feel. Feelings are trying to teach us something, to give us very critical and valuable information about our lives.

Common Belief # 6: 'I have to feel 'good' at all times': A great myth in our world today is that we must experience only feelings we judge to be positive or good. If we feel sad, angry, fearful, we must immediately do something to feel 'better'. Unfortunately, what this does is create an emotional yo-yo effect.

If you have feelings surfacing, and you are trying to mask them, then they will come back. Now, this is not to say that you must absolutely experience everything in the moment when it arises — that is not possible with the demands in most people's lives. What it means is that you can no longer walk around believing you must feel positive and up all the time.

We cannot experience joy without giving ourselves permission to experience and work through all feelings.

To feel at all, and to feel deeply, we must accept that there will be times when we experience emotions that we find uncomfortable and even painful.

Common Belief #7: 'I must 'figure out' AND FIX how someone else feels': Do you find that there are times when you are overly focused on 'figuring out' how someone else feels? Whenever a woman spends time and energy trying to assess or analyze how someone else feels, her own time and energy are wasted. As women, we do this a great deal, and it seems to help us feel safe with the other person. Doing this is usually an outcome of our own fear regarding the other person. Asking 'why' frequently ends up with blame. With regard to human behavior and experience, asking 'why' can never find an answer, because as people have so many different motivations and experiences. Yet, we believe that if we can explain their feelings – or more often, their reactions towards us – then everything will make sense.

Proactively Experiencing Your Emotions

We are beginning to give ourselves permission to feel and express emotions. We are learning to revel in their energy, and use them advantageously each and every day. We also know that when we deny how we feel, we deny ourselves. Yet, what are they really and how can a woman learn to identify with them and feel comfortable with them in her own skin?

The types of emotional sensations that we can experience are as limitless as we are. The ones that we often judge as positive – excitement, elation, joy, and contentment – are often the ones that we have the greatest comfort with, once we allow ourselves to feel them. (The section on Abundance in chapter 9 will provide you with some direction.)

Fear, anger and sadness are the three core emotions that we identify as:

➤ Being more challenging for us to feel, experience and release, and

➤ Are the ones that we have silenced the most.

The root of all feelings that we deem negative is fear. And, living fear – based for women is incredibly common and keeps us disconnected from our true nature, and feeling powerless. Anger and sadness are offshoots of fear – at their roots – yet, are experienced differently in our bodies. Let's take a look at fear, anger, and sadness and, begin to see how we can transform them from enemies to allies.

Fear

The true purpose of fear is that it is part of our instinctual nature. It is there to tell us when danger is approaching, or when a threat to our physical safety is occurring. It is great to have this inner system that will assist us to be safe, and remain healthy in our lives. Yet, how much of the fear, anxiety and even terror that we feel through the day is connected to our survival instinct? Not much!

It is critical to know what fear is and to understand its presence and impact upon your life. Check in with your body right now. Are you feeling anxious just reading these words and thinking about fear? That is not an unusual response, and it is also an indicator that you are holding residual fear in your body. You see, your fear gets stored – not only on an emotional level, but your fear reactions to past events get stored on a cellular level. In turn, it becomes a part of your chemical makeup and becomes a part of how you function, how you think about yourself and your ability to face the challenges that you have each day.

For most women, a cloak of fear has become a garment that they wear each and every day in their lives. Having this cloak influences and guides us in detrimental ways throughout the day. Now, the intention is not to take off the cloak all-together. The reality of our lives do not believe that we, as women today, can not totally live without feeling and having physical reactions to fear. We need our instinctual fear response to help keep us physically safe, and to help us to make choices about our work and personal relationships. It is the reality at this time. But *reducing* the fear that we carry – especially the toxic fear – there will mean a lot less fear in our world.

How Fear is Reinforced

Each and every one of us has a different capacity to experience and move through fear. This can often confuse us. Sometimes, we see other people being able to push ahead through a situation that produces fear for us. Sometimes, we see people quite immobilized by their fear when we want them to simply 'get over it'. Furthermore, a person may be stuck in fear in one situation, and confident and alive even when afraid in another situation! Fear varies between individuals, and between situations.

Another confused notion we believe says that all fear is the same thing, and we need to react the same way when we experience it. Knowing the difference between anxiety, fear, and terror can help you gain perspective, and understand what you are actually experiencing. This, in turn, allows you to take charge and intervene. As with anger, a person's fear response can become a fear reaction through distorted thinking. If you experience something fearful, and focus and dwell on the fear, then you are more likely to be pulled down by your fear, unable to use your creativity and intuition to find a plan of action. Your fear is giving you a message that you need to hear, and its message can be blocked by distorted thinking.

Fear's important message can also be blocked by a 'fear of feeling fear'.

Did you know that one of the most common blocks to moving through our fear is actually the fear of feeling fear? We create a great deal of stress in our lives by the very action we take to avoid the fear! Because we are living in a time that is increasingly 'fear-based', we are required to use more and more energy to create and maintain these blocks so we can avoid fear. As a result of all this, we feel more isolated from each other and become more reactive in our rage responses. A woman may even suffer physical side effects, such as a weakened immune system. As long as people continue to avoid emotion – especially fear – this self-created trap will be maintained. Instead, by understanding anxiety and fear, and opening yourself up to the messages that they bring, you can:

▸▸ Assess what you are actually experiencing.

▸▸ Put anxiety, fear, or even terror in to perspective in the moment.

▸▸ Choose which response is most pro-active in the moment.

Anxiety, Fear and Stress

Anxiety is a generalized feeling of tension in the body that alerts you to a particular situation. It does not leave you feeling 'frozen', nor does it trigger the instinct to run. Instead anxiety stimulates your adrenal glands to secrete adrenaline that will help you 'get the job done'. Adrenaline can also produce anxiety as a way of pointing out that certain situations offer opportunities for growth.

Stress will lead you to feel more anxiety in your life, which may lead you to feel anxious and nervous all day long. It is easier to deal with anxiety if you understand that real anxiety can be linked to a particular situation or event. In fact, anxiety is often transitory in nature – when the event or situation is over and complete, the anxiety reduces. Therefore, if you feel anxiety all day throughout the day, you may have moved into living in a fear-based manner as a result of past experiences, underlying emotional and/or physical issues, or through experiencing unresolved feelings over a long period of time. Do not judge yourself for this (check in to your brain chatter right now), but simply, understand there is a difference between situational anxiety, and fear-based living.

Positive self-talk is highly effective in helping you use the anxiety to your advantage. Self-accepting statements such as *'Yes, I am anxious, so I will really need to think through my next steps,'* or *'I am feeling anxious, what is really happening?'* may assist you to feel in charge, enabling you to use your resources and go with the anxiety. Reframing your anxious thoughts with affirmations such as *'This will be over soon,'* or *'How I feel in this moment is not how I feel all of the time,'* or *'I will do the best I can in this moment,'* help you take a responsive self-coaching approach to anxiety-triggering situations.

Genuine fear is a systemic feeling of tension in the body. You may experience tightening in the chest, back, and neck, and a weakness in your knees, dry mouth, and the increased need to urinate. You may also find that you are more confused, that thinking rationally is very difficult and that this continues over a period of time, often weeks or months. Genuine fear is often more than a one-time experience. Think of a particular person who triggers fear in you. Whenever you are with that person, the reaction occurs. This is genuine fear.

Along with your fear reaction, you may become angry and aggressive, or may want to run. This is called the 'fight or flight response'*. At times, this response is very important, and you do need to run! Most often, however, the 'fight or flight response' is a very clear sign that there is something definitely not right for you in a particular situation. When you experience fear, simply ask yourself: *'What is not right for me here?'* What you have been taught about fear may encourage a 'fight or flight response' even when there really is no actual physical threat to yourself in the situation.

With regard to success, you need to be aware of the roles that anxiety, living a fear-based life, and fear can have. Know that through the experience of pursuing your dreams and goals, you will experience fear. Know that you may understand the source of how you feel, but, at times you will not. Avoid trying to 'figure out why' you are feeling a certain way. Know too that pushing through fear promotes growth and strengthens you. 'Pushing through' means assessing the situation and asking yourself the following questions:

*Term developed by Dr. Hans Selye.

▸▸ Am I anxious in this situation, or experiencing the stronger emotion of fear?

▸▸ Does my response fit with the reality of the situation?

▸▸ How are my thoughts distorting how I am feeling?

▸▸ What choice do I have in how I deal with it, and how I respond to my feeling?

Also, refer to the exercise at the end of this chapter to work with these concepts further.

Exploring Anger

Feeling anger is usually the sign that we believe something is being taken away, and therefore, connected with our fear of loss. We can believe that it is being taken from ourselves, or, from someone we feel protective of. In our families and in our culture, we have received mixed messages about anger through how we have seen it expressed. Some people use loudness or a tone of anger as their usual form of self-expression. Other people have learned that any loud expression is terrifying, and should be avoided at all cost. For many women, we have received the message that we should feel or express our anger at all costs. Knowing our beliefs and perceptions about anger is critical so we can understand anger.

Our feelings are our feelings – this is clear. What becomes unclear is how our thoughts can distort our feelings, and particularly, feelings of anger. We experience anger when we believe that something or someone could be taken away from us. As we think about it more and more, over and over, we can add to it other thoughts about the person, the situation, or any others involved. And, the more we think, the angrier we become. Through our thoughts, we then add information from the past, which increases our anger, and thoughts about the future, further confusing us. This process distorts the original pure anger we were feeling and which was providing us with useful information in the present. So, what is behind this process of distortion? Fear is. As we think more about our anger, we begin to feel angrier, and more 'out of control', and scared.

Also, through this process of distortion, we lose the clarity of anger. In its purest form, anger has a particular clarity. It provides an amazing form of energy, which motivates us to solve the problem at hand. It provides the focus to use our creativity in finding and implementing that solution. Anger brings amazing force, and, when we know and accept the anger we feel, we can harness this energy and use it for the highest good of others and ourselves!

Choosing how you respond when feeling anger is the key, and choosing how you channel the energy created can lead to amazing solutions!

Exploring Sadness

Sadness is the feeling experienced after a loss. It is easy to relate sadness to the death of a person, but sadness can also be experienced whenever you lose anyone to whom you've had a connection. Connection is vital to us as humans, for through connection, we experience who we are and receive recognition from others. Connection provides us with the fuel for personal growth and development. Being connected to others is required for life.

> **When a person leaves your life, you need to grieve the loss of their presence and recognition you gained through your relationship with them. You need to grieve how 'I' was reflected through them.**

Our pain will also reflect that we have lost the 'potential' recognition, and love we believed they could give us. Unfortunately, denial of sadness is also on the rise. We believe we need to be 'happy' all the time, and that any other emotion should be rejected. We believe that if a person is sad, she or he must be cheered up. We also believe that sadness and the expression of sadness are more acceptable for women than for men. Yet, even women should only experience and express sadness on a time-limited basis, and in as concealed a manner as possible. We need to now see our tears now as a sign of strength, and not weakness, for we have the courage to express how we feel.

As with anger, fear, and all other emotional experiences, energy is created. When this emotional energy is not expressed and moved through externally, it turns inward and contributes to mental and physical illness. Sadness is also connected to personal growth. When you come to a new level of self-awareness and greater self-esteem, you may find that you look back on some of your actions and relationships, and feel sadness over choices you have made, or how you have treated certain people. When you experience this type of sadness, it really is a wonderful gift. This type of sadness lets you know that you do not have to keep creating remorse, but can now be pro-active – living your life and relationships with love and integrity. This type of sadness also gives you concrete evidence that you are learning, and growing, and becoming more of the esteemed person that you deserve to be.

Whenever you carry unexpressed sadness connected to a past event or relationship, the feeling remains buried inside, and the precious energy that you need to live your life fully today is siphoned to the past – like gasoline being stolen from a gas tank. Find a way to bring closure to the past. This will allow you to let go of the negative impact that sadness has on you in the present.

> 'Closure' does not mean rejecting the memory of the person nor the joy experienced in knowing them. Closure is acknowledging, owning, and expressing the feelings you have – and letting go of their ongoing negative impact.

Trust that you will know when the time is right for such a letting go. The ultimate goal of closure is to release you from fear surrounding your sadness. There are may excellent tools for assisting with closure – writing, artistic expression, concluding unfinished business, developing a meaningful ritual, seeking help from others and many more. Your options are as creative as you are!

There are two important things to be aware of with regard to sadness. First is the duration and depth of your feeling. If you find that expressing your sadness does not bring relief and/or you are sad over a long period of time, you may actually be experiencing grief or depression. Second is whether you are 'overly sad' for someone else and their experience. (One telltale sign is thinking of them nearly all day, in a state of feeling 'how' they feel.) It is easy for caring, sensitive people to carry someone else's sadness for them. Know that it is their sadness for them to experience, as part of their life learning, and not yours. Listen for your intuition telling you when you are experiencing too much of their sadness for them – be empathetic and caring, rather than feeling it for them.

One of the most common errors around feelings is how people confuse sadness and depression. Sadness and depression are different but related experiences. We often use the words 'I feel depressed' to describe a variety of emotions, masking how we are truly feeling. Yet the words 'sadness' and 'depression' are often used interchangeably to describe how a person feels. Remember that sadness is what we feel about a real or perceived loss. Depression is a day-to-day state of emotional being which continues 'without relief'.

In part, depression arises from unexpressed sadness and other unexpressed emotions. But, there is also a physiological or body-based component to depression. Research today is actively discovering physical susceptibilities related to genetics, body chemistry and general health, food sensitivities, and environmental toxins, to name a few. Treatment for depression often includes looking at the cause of the depressive symptoms, and at how the depression manifests in an individual's life. Medication or natural remedies are often used. But, a large piece may be missing from this approach – owning and experiencing how these feelings get addressed. This varies from person to person, and, according to the severity of their depression. But, it is vital that they be addressed.

Exercise: Overcoming Fear

If you find that you are experiencing fear, the following exercise will help you think through it and shift its hold upon you. Know that you are in charge!

1)   Think of a person to whom you have a fear reaction. Assess if you really need that person or situation in your life. If yes, how you can change the nature of your relationship with them? How can you shift your thinking so they do not have such a hold over you? How can you change the nature and the duration of the time spent with them?

_____

_____

_____

_____

_____

_____

2) Become an observer of your fear response, and be aware of when and how it occurs. Ask yourself, *'Is distorted thinking increasing the fear I am experiencing?' 'Am I having a fear of fear reaction?'* Then ask yourself, 'Is fear the real feeling, or am I feeling something else?'

_____

_____

_____

_____

_____

_____

3) Use positive self-talk to help you to accept that you are feeling afraid. Use it to also assess whether there really is anything to be afraid of in this particular situation, and if not, use positive self-talk to reassure yourself there is actually nothing to fear.

_____

_____

_____

_____

_____

_____

Guilt and How to Conquer It!

Over and over, women ask about guilt and how to get rid of it in their lives. Many women find that their lives are influenced, and sometimes even ruled by feelings of guilt - whether it is about the quality of the work they are doing, their roles as spouses, mothers and caregivers, or even with regard to how they feel about themselves each and every day. A woman is not able to embrace energy choicing in her life, nor, be able to fully focus on her goals until she understands what guilt is really all about.

It is as though she is covered in a heavy weight that stops a woman's ability to function on all levels. It usually occurs as the outcome of an interaction with someone else, and our families are especially good at pushing that button that starts the feeling of guilt. Yet, as women, we actually create the feelings of guilt we have through our self-defeating thinking and through believing that we are ultimately responsible for the feelings, challenges and problems of others.

> **We also 'guilt' ourselves – have you ever eaten a decadent dessert and, all the time you were eating, your brain chatter went on and on about how you shouldn't be eating it?**

Let's look at what guilt really is all about, and how we have learned to use it. We do need to have the feeling that comes along with experiencing guilt, as long as it fits with having a conscience. It is appropriate to feel guilt, say, if you physically hurt someone, have an affair, or break the law. This experience of guilt is the outcome of having a conscience. And, this experience keeps us all from living in total anarchy. It keeps the laws and the social rules and norms in order, with us believing and following them. If you think about how often you feel guilt, what percentage of the time does it fit the definition above? Hopefully, very rarely! Yet, as women, we feel so much guilt. In

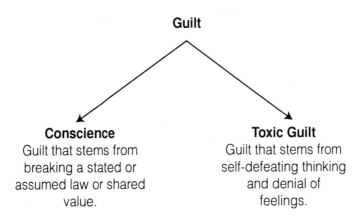

Guilt

Conscience
Guilt that stems from
breaking a stated or
assumed law or shared
value.

Toxic Guilt
Guilt that stems from
self-defeating thinking
and denial of
feelings.

actuality, our feeling guilt is a learned experience. It is something that we have learned to do in ourselves, and accepted as the way that we must feel in life.

The bottom line is that we have learned to feel guilt rather than to admit and own how we are truly feeling. It is closely tied to shame, and how we have not learned to know and state what we really want and need. We feel guilt when we break the laws that we believe we are 'supposed to' follow in our lives. Others who are close to us know how to push the button so well, because they know us so well. They can push our guilt triggers as a way to cloud the issues at hand, and as long as we allow ourselves to be ruled by guilt, chances are excellent that it will keep being a powerful force in our lives.

To better understand guilt, it is helpful to look at the difference between non-toxic and toxic guilt. Let's first review what is '**non-toxic**' **guilt**. This is the feeling of discomfort that we normally feel when we break a law. It is our normal reaction to having a conscience, morals and values. Conscience kicks in when we break one of those internally understood laws. We get the internal message that it is wrong, and use this as a guide for how to live our lives. We must have this conscience to maintain a certain societal structure or way of life. Unfortunately, for many women, 'how' they have learned to view these laws and their experience of the guilt falls in the category of 'toxic guilt'.

The second type is 'toxic guilt'. It is a guilt that most women feel on a daily, almost continual basis that has begun to feel like a normal part of life. You see, we as women have learned to feel this type of guilt.

If you experience guilt in your life on a daily basis, most likely it is toxic guilt that you are experiencing. Let's look at one of the primary sources of this learning. Our grandmothers and mothers were living in a time when they were not allowed to be all they could be. They were only allowed to have their own thoughts, desires and wishes, and make choices on a very limited basis. They had learned that they were supposed to give away themselves to keep the social order running, and to keep intact the rules that men and women had learned about their roles in life.

To be able to do this, they had to learn toxic guilt. They had to learn to have this horrible, constricting feeling inside of them come up whenever they had a thought or a desire which did not fit with the rules of the day. It is the way it was, and it was not right. We were raised and nurtured by women who believed in this old order, but we cannot blame them for how we feel toxic guilt today. We are in a new time,where all these old rules for living must go out the window. We are also living in a new time where choice, and the need to make choices, is present in our lives on a daily basis. Yet, what we are doing is still following the old guilt-based way of living. Putting this old belief together with the fact that we are living faster paced, more stress-filled lives, plants the seeds for guilt to flourish and grow. This type of guilt is toxic, as it harms our physical, mental, emotional and spiritual well-being. It robs us of energy that can be directed to our goals. We can allow ourselves to feel guilt about anyone and anything we try to accomplish in the day – and always feel inadequate in doing it.

The next time you feel this wave of guilt strike, ask yourself the following questions (there is space at the end of this chapter for your responses):

"How do I feel about this situation right now?":
Ask this when guilt arises with regard to you
interacting with someone, when you find you cannot
keep up with life's demands, or even when you are
simply feeling down or inadequate. You see, guilt
remains as long as you do not acknowledge how you
truly feel. When you really allow yourself to admit how
you are feeling, and feel it, guilt begins to diminish and
evaporate.

"What choice do I have right now?": This second
question is very important, especially if you are having
difficulty getting in touch with how you truly feel
about the situation. This is a very powerful question as
it can shine light on an ongoing life problem. Do you
not feel that you have choice with regard to a particular
person? Dig deeper in yourself to seek the answer.
Often, guilt and feeling like there is no choice go hand
in hand with regard to a significant other in your life.
And the moment that you do not believe that you have
any choice is the moment when the door is shut on
having choice. Remember that your body believes
whatever your brain tells it – and the same goes for
believing if you have choice or not. And then the feeling
in your body is that of being trapped. As soon as you
recognize and admit to how you feel, ask this next
question.

"What do I really want to do right now?": Asking
this question taps into both your genuine needs and
desires as well as your intuition. It may not be an easy
question to ask, as you don't often ask it of yourself. You
may find that your mind wanders to the needs and
desires of others. In response, refocus on yourself and ask

the question again. Really be open to hearing the answer, and it will come through clearly for you.

You may be wondering, what will asking these questions change? The first one that focuses on how you feel lets you take a step back from the feelings of guilt, and tune in to how you are really feeling. You disentangle from the guilt, so you can honestly assess the situation and how you really want to use your energy. Asking yourself how you feel in the moment also pulls you out of self-defeating thinking that keeps the guilt alive. Asking the second question about choices keeps you in the moment and helps you make really great decisions about how you do or don't want to use your energy to deal with a particular situation. Then, when you ask yourself what you want to do, and listen to the response, you use the energy of healthy selfishness to give yourself further distance from the guilt, and a greater understanding of your needs and desires.

Even if you are thinking that asking these questions won't make a difference, and that you still have to follow through with certain jobs or tasks, asking these questions will get you out of the energy stealing and stress producing mode of guilt. Remember that toxic guilt robs you of your personal power and belief that you have choice. Disconnecting from it helps you see the bigger picture, and how you use your energy. The following exercise provides the space for you to work with these three powerful questions when feeling plagued by guilt.

Exercise: Undoing Guilt's Power

Use the following space to answer these three questions:

1)   How Do I Feel about this Situation Right Now?

_____

_____

_____

_____

_____

_____

2)   What Choice Do I have Right Now?

_____

_____

_____

_____

_____

_____

3)   What *Do* I really want to *Do* Right Now?

_____

_____

_____

_____

_____

_____

The idea has gained currency that women have often been handicapped not only by the fear of failure, but by the fear of success as well.

- Sonya Rudikoff, writer

Chapter 8

Intuition and Personal Power

**Intuition and Creativity are a woman's
greatest success allies.**

Intuition is the key that unlocks the door for true success, inner peace and personal power in life. For a woman to be able to own, listen to, and nurture her intuition is also the key for feeling whole inside herself. It is part of the foundation that says 'yes, my life makes sense for me' and how 'I live my life is based on the truth that comes from my inner core'. Intuition's purpose is to provide us with information and support with regard to changes we may be making, or the direction in which we are taking our lives. Know that it is not a magical power. It is a part of who we are. Intuition is an incredibly powerful gift given to us to help us through life.

Being connected to, and using, our intuition to the max is necessary today. Unfortunately, with our lifestyles and pace of life, many women are more disconnected from their inner knowing and, ultimately, their inner resources and power than ever before. And, no woman can deny that she needs all the help that she can get! Think of a woman who you consider to be wise, a woman who you go to, or think of, when you need that extra help and support. She is a woman who has lived her life connected to, and living through, her own inner knowing.

Intuition is the most naturally present and accessible tool available to us. We have not learned how to tune in to the awesome information and direction available to us on a regular basis, rather we have learned to deny it and tried to shut it down. This learning has come through being taught to believe that we are not supposed to be powerful and successful women who are in charge of our lives. No wonder we have been taught to deny our inner knowing, and sometimes, feel ashamed of our intuition's awesome ability.

> **Intuition is experienced as the inner awareness of something that you are not able to talk yourself out of.**

It can be that 'uh-oh' feeling that comes up when you meet someone for the first time. It is that flash of insight you have about how to deal with a particular situation. It is that little voice that whispers in your ear saying you need a second opinion. It can be that nagging feeling in your gut that something is not right with the current situation. It is that 'light-bulb' moment that you have when dealing with a challenge, and desiring to find a solution. No matter how hard you try to deny or rationalize your inner knowing, it keeps coming back in to your awareness.

What is Intuition?

These aspects describe how we experience our intuitive knowing in daily life. Yet, what is it really? Intuition is the manifestation of our soul self at work. Intuition is the energetic essence of who we are, providing us information, direction and guidance for thriving each day.

> Intuition is the doorway for our own 'higher self' – the wisest part of who we are – to be fully present and continually active. In other words, intuition is the spiritually guided energy gifted to us to help us live

> our life purpose, and complete the
> lessons we are here to learn. It is the
> experience of God's breath in us that
> urges us to be the best we can be, for
> ourselves, and for others.

Intuition is a spiritual connection. It is the line of communication between the Higher Power and us. The purpose of our soul is to be the receiver and amplifier of this knowledge. The purpose of our body is to be the listener and the responder to this knowledge. Our job is to enable the channel through which intuition flows to be as open as possible.

Recognizing and Experiencing Intuition

Each and every one of us has intuitive experiences on a daily basis. Yet, most people have never learned to recognize when their intuitive knowing is at work. When this energetic force goes unrecognized, it fails to grow. Some people may have learned to believe that they do not have any intuition – that this inner knowing does not exist for them. This is a learned belief that is simply not true. Each of us is born with intuitive ability, but if it is not acknowledged and nurtured at an early age, and used through our lives, our intuition does not develop to its true potential.

Both women and men are intuitive, but some people naturally have more. So, it is important not to compare how much 'gut instinct' you have to others. The beauty of it is that it can be enhanced and developed in everyone. What is so wonderful about this inner knowing is that it may feel small or even non-existent, but it never truly leaves. Know that it is waiting for you deep down inside.

> Imagine that intuition looks like an
> excited child in a classroom,
> waiving her arm and waiting to be

called on by the teacher. Waiting for
you to call on her.

Instinct and intuition originate from the same source, but with slight differences. Instinct is based in our biological make-up. The purpose of instinct is to ensure the survival of the human race. It often determines how we react when faced with a situation that threatens us on a very basic level of survival, safety, and personal growth. Intuition is more fully a personal spiritual force. It acts as a guidance system that can enhance our quality of life, and become a catalyst for personal growth.

All living beings are born with intuitive ability that can be as simple as the survival mechanism of instinct, or have limitless potential of intuitive wisdom, as with humans. Women and men have intuitive ability, yet there is a difference in the quality of it for women. This difference gives us access to a greater, natural intuitive ability. Consider this a 'package deal' that came with your uterus! This heightened ability ensures the survival of the next generation. Most women have experienced 'knowing' that danger is near throughout their immediate surroundings and have been able to act to prevent someone from getting hurt. Women who are mothers know what it is like to awaken suddenly in the night to a quiet house (and experience a little frustration over this) and, shortly afterward, hear their child who has awakened in need. Know, that for those of you who no longer have your uterus as a result of surgery, this extra intuitive energy is still with you!

Experiencing Intuition

There are similarities in how each of us experience intuition, yet intuition is, by nature, also very personal and individualized. You can learn the common signs and sensations to recognize when your intuitive knowing kicks in, yet only you can learn your own patterns and how intuition feels as it happens in your body. Each person has his or her primary form of experiencing it. Some of us are more body-oriented, and know when our intuition is happening through goose bumps, a sense of inner heaviness, or a tingling feeling. At times, some find their body awareness so strong that they become immobilized for a moment. Others identify certain thought patterns as their cue that their intuition is working. Others experience it as a little voice speaking in their ear, or as pictures that arise on the 'inner screen' in their mind's eye.

People often ask, what is the difference between brain chatter and intuition? In a previous chapter, we have learned that 'brain chatter' or self-defeating thinking is that inner dialogue that you have with yourself that seems to have a life of its own. The depleting effects of brain chatter on your body were identified. Intuition may come through in your brain chatter at times, yet it does not carry the same draining feeling of heaviness as brain chatter. It brings a lighter sensation with it; you know that its intent is to help you, not to put you down.

Yet a woman can be an expert at shutting down her intuition. First, you have a sense in your body that is different from how you are feeling. It may feel like a twinge or a pull in your awareness. You may even have goose bumps or experience or have an 'uh-oh' feeling arise in your body. The key is to recognize and own your experience in the moment, trusting that you are being provided with this awareness for a purpose. Instead, what we often do is 'flip' in to our brain chatter, as we do not 'understand' what we are experiencing. You see, we believe that we need to logically and rationally make sense of whatever we are experiencing for it to be true. We experience intuition in our bodies, and then, jump to our brain and begin thinking and thinking about it. Doing this shuts off the sensation, which, in turn, denies the information intuition is providing us.

In this process what happens is two-fold:

▸▸ First, we react to what we are experiencing in our bodies, and

▸▸ Secondly, judge it, feel some fear and in turn shut off or minimize the information that our intuition is attempting to provide for us.

All in all, intuition only feels negative when we judge it that way which tends to happen when we do not want to hear what it is saying. Judging intuitive knowing stems from fear. However, intuition may come through during brain chatter for, at times, it is the only way your intuition can get your attention! As you learn other ways to hear your inner knowing, intuition based brain chatter will be reduced.

The Benefits of Strengthened Intuition

Let's be honest. As a result of the way we are living our lives today, we often experience only fleeting moments of feeling in charge of our lives. We expend most of our energies responding to the needs and demands of others. We may have visions and goals for our lives, yet often feel so engulfed by the desires of others that our desires get put on the back burner. It can feel like a continual siphoning of energy, leaving us trying to control others, rather than living in charge.

> By choosing to open up to your intuition and listening and responding to her wisdom your sense of personal power begins to shift and rapidly grows.

Tune in to your body at this moment. Is your inner dialogue or brain chatter questioning if this really could work? Do you doubt that you can live in charge of your own life? Are you experiencing some confusion, or feeling some anxiety right now? All of these reactions are normal. Living in charge from your inner knowing challenges how you – and most people – live their lives today. Know that you are awakening a deep inner wisdom that will connect you with your personal power.

Understanding the incredible benefits available to each and every one of us may assist you in getting past any unease you may be experiencing. You see, intuitive knowing will challenge you to think about a particular situation, your life and yourself in a different way. As a society, we have invested a lot of time and energy in creating our lives in a certain way, living particular lifestyles, following certain patterns in our day and having particular beliefs about how we should live. Living with your intuition fully alive and working for you challenges the status quo, and opens the door for change, personal growth and living a life that has meaning for you.

> We work hard to follow the belief that we have to live life a certain way and follow the rules and beliefs that others have told us are right for us in order to be successful. This has kept us 'boxed in' and believing in something which may not be our inner truth.

Intuition provides information and support to assist with challenges and change. A common experience for a woman is to develop a plan, and come up with an innovative idea that she would like to implement. When she begins to express it to others, she is met with resistance from others who she thought would be supportive. What happens next is that she questions her own creative idea, and can even begin to take what she perceives to be a personal challenge, and begins to doubt herself. Having greater personal power through intuition, and really owning her inner wisdom, would provide her with a source of continual inner support and reinforcement for her idea and perspective.

Incredible benefits accrue to self-esteem through developing intuition. Through noticing, observing, acknowledging, using, and giving credit to your intuition, your relationship with yourself rapidly develops. Each time you ask yourself for your opinion and listen to what you hear, self-esteem is given a boost. Building your intuition can also help reduce stress.

Living more intuitively will not free you from life's ups and downs, but will give you a better sense of which choices are for your highest good. You will spend less energy thinking about what to do, or what choices to make, and struggling over your decisions. Recall that intuition is an inner knowing that you cannot talk yourself out of, so, through relying on it, energy isn't wasted through the process of indecision. One of the greatest benefits to developing your intuition and using it as a guide in life is that you gain wisdom.

Wisdom is the outcome of listening to, trusting, and following intuition over and over again.

Intuition is also directly linked to joy. Being able to 'hear' intuitive direction can lead you to notice and experience joy in your life on a daily basis. It can be the nudge that stops you in mid-stream, makes you lift your head and notice what is amazing around you here and now. (Refer to 'the Joy Frequency' found in the next chapter.)

For women, the change is living life feeling in charge of our energy and how to use it. It enables us to find solutions to problems which are more creative and suited to who we really are. It helps us to look at our choices, so that they have meaning for us in our lives. It nudges us to look at ourselves as women who want to be present and feel alive, rather than living as 'doing machines'. Oh yes, our intuition presents us with incredible help, and also challenges our growth. The benefit of living with our inner knowing as strong and vibrant as possible drastically outweighs the temporary discomfort that is felt as a part of personal growth.

10 Truths About Intuition

1) Intuition is an inner knowing that you are not able to talk yourself out of.

2) We all have this inner knowing – both men and women.

3) Intuition is a gift and a part of you, which helps you through life.

4) Intuition may be experienced as a sensation, a feeling, or a thought.

5) Some people have a greater natural ability, yet for all of us, intuition can be expanded and enhanced.

6) Intuition is minimized, or even laughed at in our world, because this inner knowing may not appear logical or rational.

7) You may feel anxiety when intuitive messages arise, as they are trying to tell you something that does not fit with what you already believe. Intuitive knowing challenges you to live a life with real meaning for you.

8) When intuition is followed and a positive outcome is experienced, intuition is rarely given the credit.

9) You can easily get to know your intuition through being spontaneous.

10) Living more intuitively enhances your link to the Divine, and gives life greater spiritual meaning.

Self-Talk for Expanding Intuition

The following three-point program works with building on your relationship with yourself through affirming self-talk. Using these strategies in your daily life will quickly expand your intuition and increase your ability to be more in charge in your life. The three steps are:

▶▶ Step #1: Tell your intuition that you want to hear it

▶▶ Step # 2: Ask yourself for advice

▶▶ Step # 3: Move to Action

Step #1: Tell your intuition that you want to hear it: Remember, your intuition is like that eager child in the classroom, waiting to be called upon. Your intuition will come through more clearly when it knows that you want to hear it and you are committed to the knowledge that it holds for you. When you wake up in the morning, before getting out of bed say the following to yourself three times:

'I believe and trust in my inner knowing
and want to hear her as clearly
as possible today'.

Repeat this phrase through the day, whenever you think of it. Be spontaneous with this affirmation: being spontaneous is a very powerful way to reawaken your intuitive knowing.

Step # 2: Ask yourself for advice: We spend a great deal of time asking and depending upon the advice of others. We rarely ask ourselves for advice. Who better to know what is right for us in our lives than us? When faced with a concern or problem ask yourself:

'What are the alternatives for me?'

If you find that brain chatter starts and you are judging your thoughts, know that it is your fear arising. Push through this fear by asking again "What are the alternatives for me?" and, at the same time, notice how you feel in your body. You will notice that all of your energy and attention is centred on your brain, and you may even have stopped breathing! Move the focus of your attention from your head to your lower abdomen or gut. Getting out of the brain chatter and the limiting energy that goes on with brain chatter is crucial.

Ask yourself the same question again in a tone that says that you are open to hearing your intuition. When you get alternatives, there is a second question to ask. It is:

'What is the best alternative for me and my highest good?'

Be aware of any fear that creeps in when you hear the response. Know that you can also ask yourself how to put this into place, or how to most creatively work with this alternative to help with the current concern or challenge. Remember that listening to your intuitive knowing does not mean 'throwing all caution to the wind'. It means that, for your life, you have:

▶▶ More effective tools to use,

▶▶ Alternative approaches for conquering challenges, and

▶▶ Greater awareness of which direction to take that best fits for you.

Step # 3: Move to Action: Recall that intuition is an inner knowing which you cannot talk yourself out of. No matter how much you try, it keeps returning. Intuition knows when you are taking it seriously and when you really want its help in your life, when you move to action. This means acting upon and with your inner knowledge. The following 'how-to' steps will help with being more intuitive in your life. They are:

▸ Part A – "I" Decisions,

▸ Part B – Acting Upon Intuition and Significant Others

▸ Part C – Timing and Moving to Action

Part A -'I' Decisions: You've already learned the power of asking the question "What is the best alternative for me and my highest good?" At times asking this question and following the direction that you receive will be more easily done than at other times. Yet, whenever you ask this question, you energetically turn the solution to yourself, and validate your intuition by asking it for help. Even before acting upon it, these "I" decisions strengthen your inner knowing.

Sometimes, intuitive knowing is not logical in the moment. And, it may not even seem to you and particularly to others to be the 'best' move or solution. Only after following it and experiencing the outcome, can you discover that this is indeed the best alternative for 'you'. Know that you can break change into small pieces. Sometimes steps can seem so small that you may not value them. Yet, they are critical. Follow the energy of your inner knowing. When you try to shut down its energy, you create negativity in yourself, and roadblocks in your life. Only after following it and seeing the outcome, then it is revealed that this is the best alternative for 'me'.

Part B: Acting Upon Intuition and Significant Others: Intuitive knowing becomes more challenging to move into action when others are clearly involved. This is particularly clear when you are expressing, your inner knowing to someone else, especially someone with whom you have a significant relationship. This difficulty arises because:

> **Expressing your intuitive knowing is a very public expression of your own personal power. Some people in your life are going to resist seeing**

> you change, and resist the strength
> you gain through owning your
> personal power. Remember that
> most people really do not want you
> to be a strong women.

Fear arises as an outcome of our own beliefs about expressing our inner truth, or what we want or need. Fear of risk-taking can stop you from moving into action with your intuition. Remember that using your intuition does not mean that you 'throw all caution to the wind', or give up everything on the roll of a dice. Risk-taking means using your intuitive knowing and its spiritual guidance while looking at the bigger picture. Women have not consistently learned to express their opinions, or what they need, in a clear manner. Living more powerfully from your inner self will challenge you to learn how to speak your inner truth in a more dynamic and effective way.

The flip side of this is being aware that, when you delay using your intuition because you are fearful of expressing it, you could be hurting yourself and definitely wasting your energy. Most women have had the experience of being in a personal relationship with someone who is controlling or verbally abusive. Your inner voice says *'leave now'*, or *'stop seeing this person'*. At the same time, fear keeps you from ending the relationship or leaving. The problem is that when they are unwilling to learn and change, and you remain personally involved, your inner strength continues to be weakened, as this type of person wants to take all your energy and confidence so that they feel stronger. They continue to suck your energy, and you feel exhausted. Moving to action and trusting your inner voice in changing your relationship with this type of person is critical.

Often, intuition will come through clearly when dealing with a person who is controlling, or aggressive, or who only want to use you or your energy. When this occurs, your intuition often comes through in a very loud manner. Loud can mean what you actually hear. It is also about how it feels very 'loud' in your body. It is a feeling of warning or dread that can be simply described as an 'Uh-oh'. It is a strong sense that something is very wrong for you with this person, or in this situation, so your body is warning you in a very clear manner. If you are in a personal or working relationship with someone who is like this, then you may be experiencing 'Uh-oh's' all day long. If this is occurring, you may be trying to not listen to them, and use a lot of energy in doing so. And, as a result of the discomfort you feel, and the lack of understanding of what it is trying to tell you, you may try to ignore its information.

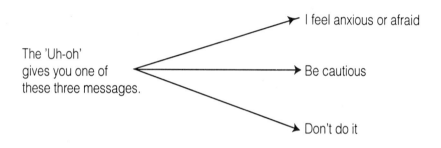

What the 'Uh-oh' feeling is trying to tell you falls into three levels:

Level 1 - "Feeling anxious or afraid": *This is a first level warning about a person or situation that your intuition is*

giving you. There is something amiss so that anxiety is being triggered in your body, and you are aware of it. Notice your brain chatter when you have this awareness. At this point, two different types of inner talking may occur. If you experience the one that says that you are making up your feelings, or trying to justify what the other person is doing, then you are ignoring your inner warning system. Notice how this type of chatter feels — it will feel like a put-down to yourself, or even drain you of your energy. The second type of inner dialogue you hear may be one to help you get through this type of situation. It is affirming in nature, giving you positive information and support that confirms or agrees with your inner knowing about this person or situation. You do not blame yourself for feeling anxious and afraid. You know that this is your inner radar telling you to protect yourself emotionally, and really work with setting boundaries and limits with this person and situation. This inner warning system may tell you that having a relationship with this person is not in your best interest, and will stop you from being all you can be.

Level 2 - Be Cautious: *The next type of 'Uh-oh' experience is stronger in nature. It is a stronger feeling of fear or anxiety, or clearer words that you hear telling you to be cautious of the person or situation. The bottom line is that there is some element of personal or emotional danger present. You may feel it when you meet a person for the first time, even though you had heard great things about him or her previously. It often occurs when dealing with a person who has been hurtful of you in the past. Your intuition could be telling you several things, such as not to trust the person or the situation. It is very important to ask yourself ' What is really happening here?' and 'Am I safe in this situation?' In this way, you can assess the potential difficulty for yourself, and choose how you will take care of yourself in the situation if you need to go ahead.*

Level 3 – Don't do it!: *This strongest level of intuitive warning usually comes through loud and clear. It means that the person or situation is not safe for you. Even though this may come to you and you hear or experience fear over and over again, you may still try to override and deny it. It may be so strong that you are actually immobilized and unable to move, yet, as women, we can be very determined to deny our personal safety and push on. Listen to this strong knowing, and avoid the situation or protect yourself. Put yourself first!*

Part C – Timing and Moving to Action: Your timing is an important factor in moving to action. You have choice in this. Simply because you 'know' the best alternative does not mean you have to jump in immediately. Know that there will be times when your intuition says 'do nothing at all', even though you are feeling the need to do something different or make a move immediately. This is a common conflict when inner fear arises and when faced with a challenge or learning that is difficult.

Know that, some times, your intuition will tell you to 'stay put' and persevere.

Remember, it is your choice as to how you will follow your intuition. You can even break the steps into little pieces - even steps so small that you think they cannot be valuable. Yet, they are critical. The force of your intuitive energy flows most easily and readily in our bodies when we connect with and listen to it. When we ignore it and try to shut down the energy, then negativity and energy blocks are created in the body.

Spontaneity is one of the most powerful ways to quickly enhance your intuitive abilities. When you are spontaneous, you go with the energy of the moment. Most of us live in the past (guilt), or the future (worry), and rarely know what it means to live in the moment. Being spontaneous teaches you how. What does it mean? It means acting on an idea or impulse that feels like it is the absolute right thing for your highest good in any given moment.

Have you ever been driving on a regular route, and knew that you needed to turn left rather than go forward, and later found out that you missed a huge accident? Or, have you ever spoken with a stranger in a crowd, and really learned something important from them? Have you ever reached out and touched or hugged someone, without thinking about it first? These are wonderful examples of spontaneous acts that can really make a difference in your life, even if the difference is simply experiencing a joy moment or one that takes you out of your daily routine.

Sometimes, being spontaneous may not seem that it has a great outcome, especially when you are judged or rejected by someone else for our actions. When this happens, take a look at the bigger picture. Through being spontaneous, you may have learned something that you really needed to know or experience for your personal growth, and know that any act of spontaneity assures your intuition that you are listening to it and its guidance.

For your highest good is the key when it comes to being spontaneous

Am I Being Spontaneous or Impulsive?

Being human, we often do impulsive things that really are not in our best interest. Impulsive acts are those that give us pleasure for the moment, and we certainly do need them in our lives. Yet as women, we often choose things that are detrimental to us and undermine proactive self-care. Examples include overeating, consuming alcohol to excess, talking about others in a negative way or over-spending.

You may even find yourself doing something impulsive, justifying that it is your intuition at work. More often than not, it is your impulsive self that really does not have your greatest best interest at heart. Notice that being spontaneous and being impulsive come from different sources, and feel difference in the moment and at the outcome.

Am I Being Spontaneous or Impulsive?

	Source	Experience	After-experience
Spontaneous	An action, choice, or information about a possible action or choice, that comes to you suddenly. Has an element or feeling of confidence, lightness, or fun.	The energy you require flows easily and feels like absolutely the right thing to do. Focus is not on outcome but rather on the experience of spontaneous action.	Sense of feeling energized or re-energized. Can also bring peace, joy, or excitement. Even if the outcome does not appear 'right', or is judged negatively by others, you retain a sense of rightness about it at your core.
Impulsive	An act done without fore-thought, either towards the act or towards its consequences for you. Often a reaction to stress, fear, or a feeling of being overwhelmed.	Energy required may: 1) need real effort on your part, or; 2) bring a feeling of being out-of-control. Focus is on how the outcome will relieve stress or reduce anxiety/fear.	Short-term high or sense of relief or high, followed by a deep low or despair. Energy feels drained. Another search begins for the new impulsive action that will create a high again.

Keys to Jump-Starting your Intuition

Women need to have creativity in their lives – it is as necessary as the air we breathe. We are incredibly creative. Our difficulty is in not understanding that creativity is operating in our daily lives. We do not recognize it when it occurs, and we do not give ourselves credit for being creative. We are 'stuck' in the definition that being creative means we must be able to decorate a house beautifully, prepare elaborate meals, be artistic, or even have a dramatic flair. And, being 'stuck' in this limiting definition keeps us looking at other women who fit this definition with envy and even jealousy. Simply put, we are 'stuck' in another form of negative thinking about ourselves, so we continue to minimize who we are, and the amazing things we do each and every day.

> **Creativity is simply putting things together in a way that has not been put together before.**

This can be two colors or mediums as an artist would do. In most women's lives, it means putting words and phrases together in a way that gets the job done at home and work, getting yourself dressed and ready for the day in a minimal amount of time, and actually wearing clothes that match! It means being able to schedule your lives and those of family members so that you all get through each and every day. This is a really different way to look at it, isn't it? Before you continue, reflect on the last two sentences, and look at the past couple of hours in your life. Reflect on all of the things that you have accomplished, the questions that you have answered, and the problems that you have solved. (There is an exercise at the end of this chapter where you can record your observations.)

Using this definition, you can see that there are two types of creativity:

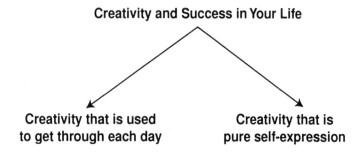

Creativity and Success in Your Life

Creativity that is used to get through each day

Creativity that is pure self-expression

Creatively Getting through Each Day: Creativity has been defined as putting two things together that have never been put together in that way before. As women, this really shows how we use our creativity to get through each and every day! Really seeing, accepting and owning this creativity is crucial for you. Being able to not minimize and deny its importance is necessary if you really want to have more energy, feel like you are in charge in your life, and focus on your goals. Commit to no longer denying that you are a creative person, and you will find your energy will immediately shift for the better.

Now, you will begin to notice how creative you are, and really owning that throughout your day. You will see how you continually reach in to yourself, and pull out something new to solve a crisis, or to make someone laugh. Notice your brain chatter, and do not allow that negative voice in your head to deny or minimize what you have accomplished. This is the time to give yourself a pat on the back. When you do this, you find that your ability to be creative increases rapidly. You will find that your intuition builds, and feels more solid, as well. Overall, you begin to really trust yourself and your instincts in your life.

> All three of these – creativity, intuition and self-trust – are three keys for you to thrive and not merely survive, in your life today.

Creativity as Self-Expression: The second type of creativity is about having a way to express ourselves in our lives that we deem as creative. Others may also label it as creative, but what is most important is that we do it for ourselves. You may be saying to yourself: "I can't do crafts, they never work out!" Well, seeing creative expression as being 'crafty' is very limiting and enables those self-defeating feelings of envy and jealousy when looking at what other people are creating. As a woman, you NEED this type of self-expression. It is about creating something with your hands that comes from your heart. You may be creating something with someone else in mind as the recipient, yet the energy from it feeds you. To build intuition and inner strength, recognize that the joy of doing it is for yourself - and when you are the recipient of what is created, even better!

Let's expand the definition of creative self-expression. The bottom line is that you have the intent to put things together in a new way that has a finished product. You may be repeating something that you made before. The key is that, in that moment, you are creating something new. Examples include: making an ice cream sundae, planting a garden, problem solving at work, rearranging furniture, coloring, sewing, writing in your journal, preparing for the holidays, painting, preparing food – the list is as limitless as you are.

The increased esteem and intuition for a woman comes through both the process of creating something new and holding the end product in her hand. Begin to notice the process you go through in creating something and you will really start to own your creative self-expression!

Tips to Enhancing Creativity: Here are some strategies for overriding your inner voice which may be saying 'I do not have the time or money' to be creative. Talk positively and confidently about taking the class or making the item that you want to create. Positive phrases that say 'I am making or doing _____' rather than 'I wish I had the time to _____' will get you mentally and energetically in the mode to let your creativity flow. If there is a specific class you want to take at a specific time, join it, write it in your calendar and let your other obligations be flexible around it. Don't put yourself last after what other people in your family want to do, or you'll never get the opportunity!

If you have unfinished projects at home, assess them, and if they no longer feel like a creative outlet for you, let them go. You may hear from others (and yourself) that you have to "finish them first" but if they are no longer feeling positive or fun, let them go. Go forward towards what does. Find someone else and create together. We are starving for connections in our lives with people with whom we can have fun. You'll find that the follow through will be easier as well.

The pre-planning it takes, the energy to implement it, the joy of the process of creation, and holding the end result, saying 'I MADE THIS' is critical to a woman's overall wellness. The energy that is generated feeds our soul, and opens up other creative avenues in our life.

It is as though you open a door to let success in to your life when you own and honor your creative nature. Attaining your other goals becomes much easier.

You will find your intuition, inner peace, confidence and ability to laugh will increase as you recognize your creativity and include it in your life. Above all, remember that you are a CREATIVELY LIMITLESS PERSON and that there are ways to turn on your creative self. Remember too that being creative is as necessary as the air you breathe, and that you are creative continually through your day.

Exercises: Igniting Your Creativity

Part 1: Creativity is simply putting things together in a way that have not been put together before. Think about, and write, all of the things that you have accomplished, the questions that you have answered, and the problems that you have solved over the last couple of hours. Try not to judge your findings – all creative acts are significant, no matter how small they may seem!

_____

_____

_____

_____

_____

_____

Part 2: Creating a 'Success Collage' is a great way to be creative and use the power of visualization to attain your goals. A collage is an outer expression of your inner experience. It is the scattered image that is created when you paste together pictures and images on a large piece of paper or poster board. A collage comes from the heart and soul – so disconnect your thoughts and do not censor what you wish to include. Be with the flow of creating your 'Success Collage' and only look at the whole picture and its meaning for you after you are done.

Suggestions for images to use:

▸▸ Pictures from magazines

▸▸ Images that you draw yourself – without self-criticism about ability

▸▸ Pieces of fabric, wool or ribbon that colorfully reflect what you want to express

▸▸ Photographs

▸▸ A symbol that reflects who you are and what success means to you.

*** Be as expressive as you can be. It is great to include the tangible things in life that you want to attain. Think 'outside the box' in terms of success, and include images that reflect how greater inner peace would feel in your life, or places that nurture your soul.

Chapter 9

Abundance, Prosperity and Success

Recognizing the abundance and joy in your life now contributes directly to your prosperity.

If you've begun to notice and experience how successful you are in your life right now, then you've also begun to see how much abundance you have in your life. The two go hand-in-hand. Abundance is not simply about acquiring goods, or having all of the bills paid. Abundance is about recognizing, owning, and reveling in all the great people, experiences, and opportunities you have right now.

Through developing a stronger relationship with yourself, another change in how you see things has probably come to your awareness. Some of those challenges in life that took so much of your focus – and worry – no longer seem to be all that important. Some of the situations and people who would create stress no longer have the power to do so. And, you have begun to do something in your life that may be new for you, or new in the depth of enjoyment that you receive. It may seem as if your senses have been heightened, and your internal radar is focusing in on what is pleasurable, rather than what is painful.

Living in the Joy Frequency

In a previous chapter, energy was addressed as being pep or stamina, and the life force energy that flows through our bodies. Joy is also a part of this energy. It reverberates with this life force. As success is attracted to you like a magnet when you shift to an inner perspective, joy is attracted to how freely your energy is allowed to flow through your body. You may have already experienced this through working with the concepts in this book.

Joy is experienced at positive, uplifting moments in life. They are peak moments and, when many of these peak moments are experienced and strung together, you begin to live a life based in happiness and inner peace. Joy is around you all of the time – you may be simply failing to give it your attention. Being able to notice the joy in life begins with acknowledging that it actually occurs.

> **As we live with increased stress and**
> **a rapid pace of life, joy has become**
> **one of the casualties of our lifestyle.**

Joy ignites by remembering it occurs – for everyone has experienced joy at some point in their childhood and adult years. Acknowledge that you are still able to feel joy, and that you want to feel it in your life everyday.

Know that brain chatter – which keeps you thinking in the past or the future – and unaddressed emotions create blocks to noticing your joy and feeling its gift. Your spirit, your genuine self wants to live by experiencing joy each day; it does not want to live tied to stress and frustration. Your genuine self knows that joy is an offshoot of feeling love, and each and every person has been designed to live life in a state of love and connection to themselves and others, not in anger and disconnection. To feel joy, all you need to do is give yourself permission to feel it.

Begin by noticing when you feel joy. Notice what pleases you, and makes you smile. When you do notice, you feel everything in your life come together peacefully for a divine moment. And, when you learn to find these joys again, you become more energized, creative, intuitive, and physically charged. You begin to lead your life appreciating those around you, and the uniqueness of whomever you meet in the day. Your ability to give and receive love increases. The other side of this is that you begin to look for the positive in yourself and others, and are even better able to deal with stress, or feelings that you may not deem as 'positive'. Feeling alive with this kind of joy is not the same as living a life that is 'rosy and perfect' all of the time.

> Being able to experience joy flows from accepting that life has both highs an lows, and from knowing that it is all about your journey of learning.

Reveling in the Abundance in your Life Now

Those little, uplifting things that happen to us are actually gifts for us in our lives. They're proof that life really is worth living. A gift is the supportive phone call you get when you're feeling blue. It's the infectious laughter heard over the din of daily bustle, and you smile. It's when you pass a produce stand, and all the colors come together in a beautiful palette. It's that moment in the day when you feel suddenly inspired, and everything that was going wrong begins to go right. It is in these moments that your body, mind and spirit truly feel aligned, and you physically experience the true connection to yourself, regardless of the pace or demands.

If these experiences are infrequent, or don't feel real when they occur, you're not alone. In this moment, as you're reading, notice how you are feeling. Try not to feel inadequate because you can't connect with the concept of these 'postcards from heaven', or the affirming energy that they bring. Know that our global belief system reinforces this disconnection by the sheer speed at which we've learned to live.

Learning to recognize, connect with, and embrace those daily gifts can provide the foundation for beginning to live in a more connected and meaningful way. When a child begins to learn to read, it is a process. She begins by simply observing pictures, noticing words, putting together those words and pictures. Then she begins to identify the words without the pictures, and begins reading when the story has meaning for her. Learning to let spiritual food in is also a process. It opens the door to our own true limitless nature and strengthens our 'success magnet'.

Opening up to the surrounding spiritual gifts can be achieved by incorporating new spiritual practices into your life, such as meditation, bodywork, yoga and experiencing nature. However, you may try different things, but still feel disconnected and discontent. To be able to pick the spiritual fruit around you, you need to let go of the internal blocks that stop your efforts. We must first unlearn the ways we block our gifts in order to relearn how to let them in. The following information is about what to work and play with during the day to help let go of these blocks. They are:

Shifting Your Perspective

Forming Your Intention

Observing Your Thoughts

Knowing Your Spiritual Leftovers

Getting Your Body Involved

Opening Up to Prosperity

1) **Shifting Your Perspective:** We often have the view that external forces will make us happy. We believe that someone or something will provide the magical solution to our internal craving for connection. To open the door to the gifts, we can shift our personal perspective or attitude, and start believing that what occurs in life flows through us, and not apart from us.

Let go of the belief that finding the right relationship or buying the right product will end your internal gnawing for connection and happiness. Having a solid relationship or enjoying your possessions can bring great pleasure, but depending on them to define who you are will keep you disconnected from the true gifts. The initial part of the process is about letting go of the belief that the outside world should feed and stimulate you. Begin to trust that there's a way for you to feel full inside (even if you don't believe it now), and beginning to understand how the gifts in your life are the food you truly need.

2) **Forming Your Intention:** This intention is about developing a conscious desire to see life's gifts, and allowing their peace and nurturing to reside within you. It's not about physically looking for them. Forming your intention is about creating a statement or a prayer through which you can ask to be more open and aware of your positive experiences. It is important and serious, but it is also play. Play with the words, and learn to trust when they come together as your own personal prayer for openness.

3) **Getting Out of Your Own Way:** As you play with this process of creating your personal prayer, you may feel some internal blocks arising. They may be experienced as anxiety or fear that could be connected to your belief about your right to feel positive and live an abundant life. Often people believe they're undeserving, and are unaware they're holding this idea. Tell yourself that you're deserving of life's gifts. And, in time, by repeating these positive thoughts, you'll notice a feeling of lightness and a greater openness to your potential.

4) **Observing Your Thoughts:** There is no faster or more effective way to close yourself to abundance than through self-defeating thinking. As you have learned in the chapter on this subject, negative thinking is any

train of thought that is directed towards yourself with the intent of undermining what you are trying to accomplish. These thoughts can take the form of fleeting ideas or brain chatter which continues throughout the day. We all think negatively about others or ourselves; it's simple human nature. But, frequent negative thinking leaves you feeling out of control. Commit to becoming gentler with yourself, and know that perfection cannot be attained. Be aware that these thoughts are ghosts from the past, particularly childhood. These thoughts block your intention of allowing daily gifts into your life.

5) **Knowing Your Spiritual Leftovers:** Many people have a story about their experience with religion that clouds their thinking of living a spiritually-based life. Be aware of your past beliefs. Living a spiritual life doesn't necessarily have anything to do with a particular religious practice, so remain open to the presence of the Divine in your life.

Regardless of your religious orientation, prayer can become a daily part of your life. It reconnects you with the spiritual energy that is all around. Even if you do not experience or feel this energy, the practice of prayer will connect you with it. An unfolding will occur where you begin to feel your connection to Spirit, and your perspective will shift so that you are more aligned with your highest inner wisdom.

Instill in yourself the core belief that each moment of your day is a form of prayer. Now I know that there are moments in each day of frustration, turmoil and worry. We are human, and we are going to react rather than respond at times. Consider these times a prayer, too, and ask yourself what is the lesson you are to learn from experiencing them.

6) **Getting Your Body Involved:** First, notice your breathing. (Most people breathe in a rapid shallow manner that cuts off the energy flow in the body, and actually gives the body the message that there is something to be anxious about.) Secondly, lift your head up, and direct your eyes upward and around you, noticing how your range of vision opens up. Lifting up your head to visually take in the gifts creates a deep,

personal knowledge of their impact. Engaging in regular meditative and stretching practices opens up your body in a new way, and clears the energy paths to allow abundant energy to flow through.

7) **Opening Up to Prosperity:** Prosperity is about good fortune, wealth, and success as defined in our world today. It is about flourishing financially. The purpose of prosperity is to provide us the basis for choice. In living and working in a materially based world, our increased ability to choose comes through having a financial freedom that goes beyond meeting our basic needs. The next section will help you to open up to prosperity as part of being a successful woman.

$ The Meaning of Money $
Money is simply a form of energy.

Money has taken on an incredible value in today's society. This value, which we have given to it, affects both women and men. It permeates and guides our thoughts, actions, and even the quality of our relationships. What has occurred is that, for many people, we no longer feel ' in charge ' of money or our finances, but rather, money is 'in control' of us.

Times have definitely changed with regard to the knowledge and time that each and every one of us needs to deal with finances in our lives. For past generations, money was much more tangible, and they did not need the investment knowledge that we need today. Even in their conversations, they did not need the same vocabulary or ability to express themselves with regard to money as we do now.

The Prosperity Process

Opening up to more prosperity in your life is a process. As your body believes whatever your brain tells it, changing how you think about money is the first step. This will enable the shift in your relationship with money to begin. As an observer of your thoughts, begin to notice how often during the day you think about money. Notice how often during the day you think about not having enough of it. Notice, too, the tension that is created in your body each and every time a thought about money moves through.

Refer to the chapter on self-defeating thinking found earlier in this book. Use the exercise there, and fit it with the thoughts that come up about money. Carry the chart on a paper with you throughout the day, and write down exactly what phrases and expressions you hear with regard to money. Write down the tone that you hear. Does it sound harsh or critical of yourself or others? Does it sound whiny and child-like with a sense of not having enough?

It is critical for you to develop an awareness of this. We often run the full gamut of self-defeating thoughts when thinking about money and prosperity each and every day. Write down your triggers as well. What starts you on this thought roller coaster with regard to money? Is it when you see someone that you think has more? Is it when you see a particular lifestyle and the possessions that they have? Is it when you look in your purse, and begin to worry about how to make it to the next pay or check? Whether you have financial abundance in your life now, or whether you find a continual lack of money in your life, as women we can still experience these self-defeating thoughts. These thoughts create a mental as well as a physical trap where we have an ongoing battle with money, and cut ourselves off from financial success.

> **Know that money is merely energy and our exchange of it is an exchange of energy. This makes it critical for a woman not to minimize the importance of the service or product that she provides and to charge accordingly.**

Truly believing this can be a challenge as our attitude is often stuck in the past with the belief that our work has no monetary value – this is what we have traditionally believed and if you are a woman working in her home as a professional homemaker, you need to begin to really value yourself and your work even when others in your life may not, and even when society does not.

Women in business can often be apologetic for the amount of money that they charge for their services, and even easily reduce fees or profits when asked to do so. Guess what? We will be challenged more on our fees by others simply because we are women. Both women and men carry the belief that the work of women does not have value, even when we are providing a key role or service. We need to immediately shift our belief about this, as others will not do it for us. The reality is, that our way of earning our living is currently based on the energy exchange of money. So how do others see the benefit of what we provide if they don't pay us what we are worth?

Becoming an observer of your thoughts is the first part of the process. Next is to reduce the amount of self-defeating thinking that you have with regard to money. Use the steps in the *Self-Defeating Thinking* exercises found earlier in this book. Really focus on committing to 'not going there' when self-defeating thoughts and worries about money want to take over. Be strong no matter how forceful or relentless they may seem. You will only rob your own power and shut down your inner 'success magnet' by doing so.

There are times when you have to think about finances, and talk with others about it as well. It is critical, in these times, to be in touch with your body, and recognize what body sensations arise. Are you feeling tense and nervous? Does a sense of inadequacy arise? Do you feel like you are in the middle of a downward spiral, and your energy is being drained? You are in charge, and know that being stuck in these feelings will simply reinforce a sense of lack in every cell of your body. For some of you, not having money is a life reality – I've been there myself in life, and know the terror that can arise. Yet, if you let the feelings and experience of it overwhelm and take over your life, you are merely reinforcing the trapped and desperate feeling that you have been experiencing.

As with all self-defeating thinking, you need to reduce and stop fighting with the negative, and then, create the garden for the positive to take root and grow. The easiest and fastest way for this to occur is to now use the power of your thoughts to your advantage. Knowing that your body believes whatever your brain tells it, it is time to shift your energy to be a force that attracts prosperity in your life. Guided imagery is the more direct and easily-accessible way for this to occur. The following two exercises will help you get in touch with your core beliefs about money, and provide tools for manifesting prosperity based upon guided imagery techniques.

Exercise 1: Assessing Your Relationship with Money

1)   Your adult relationship with money begins in childhood. What did you learn in your family of origin about money? What didn't you learn that you need to know now to be a successful woman?

_____

_____

_____

_____

_____

_____

2)   A core belief for women can be the sense of not being deserving of prosperity. It may not be something that a woman is consciously aware of, but does show up in her thoughts about money, how she views her potential, if she limits her goals, or even if she spends faster than she earns. How do you feel about being prosperous? Is there another level of feeling below what immediately pops up for you?

_____

_____

_____

_____

_____

_____

Exercise 2: Attaining Your Goals through Imagery

Remember that limitless thinking is about expanding who your are, how you think, and knowing that your potential for success and balance in your life flows from this. For this exercise, the focus is on skill building, so that you have the tools to make limitless thinking the approach you take with all challenges in your life.

Think for a moment about a particular goal you have in mind for yourself with regard to your work or your business. Can you break it down to a smaller part and work on a piece of it today? (As women, we are great at looking at the big picture, but when learning a new skill, it is not really helpful for you can easily become overwhelmed.)

The following is a step-by-step guided imagery exercise developed to help you own and manifest your dreams and goals. It is suggested that you audio record the script, and play it back to guide you through the exercise. Simply read it as it is into a recorder using a calm tone of voice. If you are not recording it, reread the exercise several times before beginning, as once you begin you are not able to refer to the words.

> **Set Up:** First, give yourself permission to take this time for yourself. Ensure that you will not be disturbed for a few minutes, which includes disconnecting your phone line, shutting the door, or telling others not to disturb you. Get comfortable in a chair that provides support for your mid-back. Close your eyes.

> **Guided Imagery Exercise** (read from this point forward if audio recording): Begin by focusing on your breath. Take three quick breaths in and out to help release tension. Next, start breathing deeply through your nose and out your mouth, exhaling any tension you may be experiencing. Check through your body, and breathe in to any areas that may feel tight or

tense. Release that tension. (Direction – leave a minute of silence on the tape to do this.)

Now turn your focus to what is going on in your mind. Is there chatter or dialogue going on? Imagine letting the voices or thoughts go in one ear and out the other. Keep reminding yourself to do this, knowing that you are not giving any energy or attention to the thoughts now. (Direction – leave a few moments of silence on the tape to do this.)

Turn your attention to your mind's eye – that part of your brain where your creative thoughts occur. If you are unsure of what this is, focus your attention on the centre of your forehead - turning all your awareness to that part of your body. (Direction – leave a few moments of silence on the tape to do this.)

In that focused space, bring to mind a dream related to your work that you have right now – a dream that you really would like to make real or a goal that you would really like to attain. You may see a clear picture of that dream, and, if you do not see a picture, tune in to your awareness and feelings about your dream. (Direction – leave a few moments of silence on the tape to do this.)

Let's move to using your five senses to help you experience your dream more fully. With your inner sight, can you see where you are? Again, if you don't see a picture, what do you sense would be there? (Direction – leave a few moments of silence on the tape to do this.)

With your inner sight, do you see anyone else there? If you don't see a picture, sense if there is the essence of anyone there. What is their energy like? (Direction – leave a few moments of silence on the tape to do this.)

Next, be aware of anything that you hear – a sound or any conversations. If it sounds very noisy, focus on separating the sounds, hearing each distinctly. (Direction – leave a few moments of silence on the tape to do this.)

Next, use your sense of smell. Is there a particular smell there? Or what smell could you add to the scene to help it best represent your dream? (Direction – leave a few moments of silence on the tape to do this.)

Can you use your sense of taste to heighten the experience of your dream? How wonderful do you think attaining this dream would taste? (Direction – leave a few moments of silence on the tape to do this.)

Now, let's use your sense of touch. Can you hold something in your hand that would represent your dream? What represents reaching your goal, and how does it feel to touch it? (Direction – leave a few moments of silence on the tape to do this.)

Take a moment to review the whole scene, and how you feel here. What is your experience of being here, and touching your dream? Experience this with your entire body and sense of self, and connect with how it feels. (Direction – leave a few moments of silence on the tape to do this).

As we are about to leave this experience of your dream, make a mental note to remember everything you can about being here. Make a mental note to remember the sights, sounds, smells, tastes and what you have touched here. Know that you will be able to recall many details, as well as how it feels to have your dream made real. (Direction – leave a few moments of silence on the tape to do this).

Now, turn your attention away from the image you have, and back to the here-and-now. Know that your dream is really yours now. It is now part of you now and you have increased your focus on attaining it. Turn your attention back to your immediate surroundings, be aware of your breathing, and begin to move slightly in your chair – take your time, especially if you are very relaxed. Open your eyes, if you have not done so already, and turn your attention to what is in the room around you. Focus on something that brings you pleasure, and gently move back in to the here-and-now. (Finish the recording here).

Immediately after completing the exercise, write down everything that you remember about visiting and being with your dream.

1)   What or whom did you see?

_____

_____

_____

_____

_____

_____

2)   What or whom did you hear?

_____

_____

_____

_____

_____

_____

3)   What smells were you aware of?

_____

_____

_____

_____

_____

_____

4)   What did you taste there?

_____

_____

_____

_____

_____

_____

5)   What did you touch or hold while being with your dream?

_____

_____

_____

_____

_____

_____

You create your reality, so the more often you do this exercise, the stronger your dream will become. You will gain a roadmap for attaining it, and, will also learn what may not really fit for you that you had thought or assumed was part of your dream.

In Conclusion

As an author, it is a real challenge to write a conclusion knowing that the information and tools found in this book will provide new beginnings for you as the reader! In closing, I'll share with you a few axioms – or truths for living – that will help you remain on course in pursuing your goals and dreams:

Living a life from your core of strength and power comes through moving from an externally experienced to an internally experienced life.

Change is becoming easier as women as a group begin to say 'I am deserving'.

We are pioneers creating a new way to live and work.

This relationship with self must be the strongest and most nurtured relationship in your life.

Qualities are about Who a person is rather than What she does.

Be able to value who you are, and all that you do, as success catapults your energy to new levels.

Success is both attaining your goal, and the journey to reach it.

Use what you are instinctually able to do for others, and do it for yourself.

Stop judging whether your goals are really important or not.

Goals and perseverance are the keys to manifesting what you desire.

*Choosing how you use your energy is the cornerstone
for being in charge.*

*Responding prevents and reduces stress.
Reacting creates and increases stress!*

*Building self-care into your daily life transforms the life that you
have to the life that you desire.*

*Observing your thoughts and reducing the self-defeating ones
immediately reduce stress and accelerate success.*

*How often are you a coach for others, and how
infrequently for yourself?*

How you think creates the reality of your life.

When you deny your feelings, you deny yourself.

*We have learned to feel guilt, rather than to admit
and own how we are truly feeling.*

Intuition and Creativity are a woman's greatest success allies.

*Wisdom is the outcome of listening to, trusting, and
following intuition over and over again.*

Remember that most people really do not want
you to be a strong women.

All three of these — creativity, intuition and self-trust — are three
keys for a woman to thrive and not merely survive in her life today.

Money is merely energy, and our exchange of it is
an exchange of energy.

Dreaming during the day feeds our souls and focuses our goals.

Thank-you for allowing me to be a catalyst on your success and life journey. All the best,

- Kathy Glover Scott

Notes

Notes

Notes

About Kathy Glover Scott

Kathy has 20 year's experience in the human service field as a manager, business owner, agency director, and psychotherapist and she holds a Masters Degree in Social Work. She is a consummate professional speaker and member of the Canadian and International Associations of Professional Speakers. Her keynote presentations and training are innovative, informative and energized – and consistently rated 'excellent' by the corporations and associations with which she works. Her topics include: the Successful Woman, Stress-Busting! and the Personal Excellence Program.

Kathy is the author of the internationally acclaimed Esteem! which contains her original model and program for building personal excellence in rapidly changing times. She is also co-editor of the Expert Women Speak Out! series. Her online courses on Esteem for Personal Excellence (3 one hour courses) and the Successful Woman (2 one hour courses) are hosted by www.learninglibrary.com

Kathy is a Reiki Grand Master/Teacher, and she is passionate about leading others to integrate higher forms of energy into their daily lives. She is married to Craig and they have two school-aged children. She lives near Ingersoll, Ontario, Canada.

You can visit her website at http://www.kathygloverscott.com or simply http://www.thesuccessfulwoman.com.